HARBOR MINISTRIES

## What Others are Saying about *Stay Wild*

"The time to give up on leading a passionate and purposeful life is not now. Tim Bohlke extends an invitation for us to reestablish a faith that is vibrant, engaged, and firmly anchored in a personal relationship with God."

-Mark Batterson,
NYT bestselling author of *The Circle Maker*

"The pace of the modern world is inherently disruptive. In the middle of all the craziness, a few sane voices rise above the noise to guide us. Meet Tim Bohlke. For decades he has been about creating places and processes for leaders to recapture inner life, purpose, and health. He understands that who we are is how we lead. If you desire to be a person who stays faithfully committed to your highest life purpose and calling, read *Stay Wild.* In it Tim will guide you to rhythms and disciplines that will ensure you live your best life."

-Dan Webster, Founder
Authentic Leadership, Inc.

"Early one Sunday morning, I was reading *Stay Wild* when my ten-year-old daughter asked if I would read out loud to her. Not expecting it to go very far, I started to read to her about the power of authentic encounters with God. Less than a week later, we finished the book together, with her leading the way. She loved the storytelling from Tim Bohlke, bridging from the scriptures to today. Since reading together, she's been asking, 'Dad, when are we going to go take some space with God? This read is more than another Christian book on how to follow God, it's an invitation to change everything. If my ten-year-old daughter can catch that, so can you."

-DJ Jergensen, Lead Pastor
Durango Vineyard Church

"Tim has stirred something deep inside me to pursue life to the full. With his unique style and simple, deep, yet practical challenges, I find myself yet again longing to break out of the ruts of average or normal. I suspect this book is also exactly what your soul is searching for to come alive and stay wild."

-Tyler Crosson, Lead Pastor
BridgePoint Church

"*Stay Wild* is a gem that struck a profound chord with me. Tim Bohlke's writing is not just thought-provoking but also deeply introspective, making it a delightful journey. Through his words, Bohlke navigates faith, creativity, and the ever-elusive quest for inner peace in our chaotic world. As someone who values faith and introspection, I found this book to be a compelling read that not only provides inspiration but also fosters a deeper connection with God. Bohlke's book provides a truly enriching and enjoyable experience for anyone on a quest for self-discovery and spiritual growth."

-Natalie Tysdal, Author and Journalist

"I highly recommend *Stay Wild.* Tim Bohlke shows us how to keep our heart for God alive and fresh even while living in a world that constantly is fighting against it. I've been involved with Harbor Ministries for the past seven years, after meeting Tim in a way that only God could have put together. I've had the privilege of seeing firsthand men's lives change by experiencing one of the Harbor Ministries groups."

-George Andrews, Wealth Advisor and Former Professional Football Player

"I have a growing concern with our culture's withdrawal into that which is safe and comfortable. It feels like we're losing our perspective on what it means to be alive. At the top of my list of concerns is the reality that you can't passionately pursue God and idolize comfort. Tim calls us as followers of Jesus to buck the cultural trends of passivity to Stay Wild in a passionate pursuit of God. I couldn't agree more, and I highly recommend this book for anyone hungry to really live this one life we've been given."

-Bryan Clark, Author of *God's Not Like That*

# Stay. Wild.

An Invitation to Pursue God
in a Fully Disrupted World

By Tim Bohlke

Stay. Wild.
An Invitation to Pursue God in a Fully Disrupted World

Published by Harbor Ministries
ISBN: 978-0-9837843-4-0



Printed in the United States

Harbor Ministries
PO Box 21984 Lincoln, NE 68542

**HarborMinistries.com**

## The Why

I have asked myself more than once *Why write another book?*

*Do I really want to enter this creative space and give the effort it requires?*

*Do I want to write it? Do I need to write it?*

*Does anyone else need to read it?*

As I wrestled with these questions during the last few months, my why came down to a destructive fire and a fisherman.

It was October 2020. The world had gone crazy. I had gathered with some guys at the Harbor anchor site in Estes Park, Colorado, including a few pastors and business leaders who badly needed to step away from the pressure and chaos and hear from God. But a destructive wildfire was building in the Rocky Mountains, the winds shifted, and just as we arrived at this newly acquired property, authorities ordered a mandatory evacuation of Estes Park.

We grabbed our gear and loaded our cars. I looked out my rearview mirror and said goodbye to a place we had worked so hard to get, wondering if I'd made a reckless decision and left the ministry exposed by investing in this property. A fire truck sat near the lodge, and soon all utilities would be shut off in the area.

We joined the long line of cars making their way out of town. We came to a near standstill on the east side of Estes, where US Highways 34 and 36 and Colorado Highway 7 converge. Emergency vehicles from Denver, Fort Collins, and Loveland streamed into the area. The afternoon skies were dark and filled with red smoke and ash. It was an eerie scene.

As we continued to move slowly, I looked to my right. I saw a guy fly fishing. He stood knee-deep, casting his fly into the Big Thompson with great rhythm. My first thought was that he was completely oblivious to everything going on around him, yet I was drawn to him. Whatever he had in that moment, I wanted it.

Then I felt the whisper:

*"This. This is why I wanted you to create a harbor. I want people to know they can find peace and a rhythm to life, even when storms are raging. I want people to know they can find strength, steadiness, resolve, and even some joy in the midst of total disruption."*

That was the image and reminder I needed for the next years of leadership and ministry. That picture of rhythm and steadiness and resolve became the why for this book and reconnected me to a personal mission and journey that continues to drive me to this day. So, now that we know my why, let's do this . . .

## Introduction

So much of parenting centers around keeping our kids safe—and often with good reason. But in our determination to keep our children (and often ourselves) safe, insulated, and comfortable, do we risk something greater? I'm convinced that most of us are determined not to risk too much, to stay back from the edge, to seek safety and comfort above all else. But what if staying back from the edge, sticking with our routines, and staying in the safe zone come at a much greater cost? What if playing it safe is the riskiest thing of all?

When our kids were younger, we took an epic family trip through Utah, the Grand Canyon, and Lake Powell. As I look back many years later, I have to say it was one of my favorite family adventures. We made so many memories. Experiencing the arches in Utah. Biking in Moab. Hiking the narrows at Zion National Park. Jet skiing on Lake Powell.

I also remember the stress.

At the North Rim of the Grand Canyon, we experienced incredible beauty. We were in awe each night at the sunsets. My wife Marcia and I were often worried about our oldest risk-taking son and his fascination with getting as close to the edge as possible. Hiking one particular trail, we spent so much time worried and frustrated with him, demanding that he get back from the edge, sometimes disagreeing about how close was too close, that we missed some moments along the way. Years later, I'm not haunted by the thought that he could have fallen. Rather, I'm haunted by regret at what we could have missed, and I wonder if we balanced the tension of risk and safety very well with him.

The world can feel like an out-of-control and unsettled place, growing more disrupted and unfamiliar each day. But this is not the time to play it safe. In this radically disrupted world that is marked by struggles and success, pain and gains, disappointments, and so much uncertainty, we need to stay wild in our faith, stay wild in our pursuit of God and others, and stay wild in investing in things that sometimes make no sense. Life is just too short to keep playing it safe. There are moments when we need to pursue the crazy, the unpredictable, the unexpected. In *The Lion, The Witch and The Wardrobe* by C.S. Lewis, young Lucy asks if Aslan (God) is safe. Mr. Beaver sagely replies, "Safe? . . . Who said anything about Safe? 'Course he isn't safe. But he's good." In our adult lives, I don't think safety is the endgame God has in mind for us.

I was recently invited to go with some guys on a multiday adventure in the British Virgin Islands. On the last night, we learned that a tropical depression was forming south of Puerto Rico. My first thought was I hope my flight out of Tortola is on time tomorrow morning. I was a newbie to the area and admit I had some premature fear about being stranded in a storm.

When I arrived at the small Caribbean airport, I learned my flight was delayed and, after waiting for a few hours, canceled. I had already missed my connection in San Juan. Now this was not a crisis, but people were concerned, trying to figure out how to get charter flights or ferries out of the area. I was way out of my comfort zone. After talking with three others, we banded together and found someone who said he had a charter flight but only four seats available. We decided it was our best option, then waited for the plane, wondering if we had been taken.

Eventually, a plane showed up, and it was not what I was expecting. The small plane was noticeably old. The pilot asked me if I wanted to sit in the co-pilot seat because it had some extra legroom. We crawled up on the wing and through a small door. The pilot's first instruction to me was, "It is going to get really hot in here so when we are going down the runway you need to hold this door open. When we make the turn for a take off, slam it shut and then hit that lock button hard because sometimes it gets stuck."

My mind was racing. The stories I'd heard from locals who had survived Hurricane Irma suddenly didn't seem so bad. I was shoulder-to-shoulder with the pilot. As we made the turn, I could not get the door locked, so with one hand on the wheel, he reached across my lap, slammed the door shut and locked it, and off we went. My anxiety ramped up, but I decided if this was it, what a way to go.

One moment early in the flight, the pilot reached to the dash to tap a dial that seemed stuck. As we entered open water on the route toward San Juan, my thoughts slowed.

*We are not promised safety in this life but we are invited to a wild, mysterious adventure with God. Don't think about the end game. Enjoy this part of the journey.*

At that moment, I began to soak in the beauty around me: an epic view of the British Virgin Islands on a clear day and water so blue you could barely tell where the horizon ended. Faced with uncertainty and risk (at least in my mind at the time), I felt alive, refreshed, and ready for what's next. If I had let the anxiety and worry win the day, I would have missed an incredible moment filled with amazing sights and a pretty good life lesson to end that great trip.

Now in my sixth decade of life, I have asked myself more than once why this stay wild idea is so compelling and why it resonates deeply with me and so many others. As I navigate what life "should" look like in this season, what does staying wild really mean? Does it look different than when I was in my twenties and thirties? Should it look different? Do some core principles remain no matter what season of life we are in? Certainly, there are physical limitations I didn't have before, but honestly, I feel like staying wild is more critical than ever.

Last fall, I took a spontaneous road trip to Boulder, Colorado, to see Marcus Mumford in the first concert of his solo tour. I remember thinking, this is not a crazy thing for my son to do in his twenties, but maybe I should act more my age. I might be the oldest dude in the theatre. Maybe I should not add to an already busy schedule. I don't need to spend the money. I should stay back, rest up, and prepare for the busy event season approaching. But at some point in the hours before that concert, I said to hell with that! I'm going.

And the truth is it was exactly what I needed. The time on the road, enjoying great pizza at The Sink, seeing Mumford along with only a few hundred other people at the iconic Fox Theatre in downtown Boulder, hearing him sing "Awake My Soul," as he stood alone on that stage, fly fishing with my son, Dylan, the next morning. It was exactly what my soul needed. The experience helped breathe life back into my weary lungs, and I entered that crazy busy stretch refreshed, awakened, and more fully alive.

Yes, staying wild is important in your twenties and thirties, but perhaps even more critical as a seasoned leader. Staying wild means embracing adventure, even doing some seemingly reckless things that may not make sense. It means embracing wonder, staying curious, exploring new places, returning to some "holy ground" places, and chasing a few cliffs along the way. For me, it means not letting age become a barrier and refusing to let culture, other people, or social and spiritual norms create limitations, define what I do or who I am or where I want to go with my life.

So yes, staying wild is crawling up on that wing and keeping that door open down the runway. It's about making an eight-hour, late-night drive to Colorado to see a two-hour concert. It's about taking others to Iceland to find a cliff that has dramatically impacted the faith journey of so many. It's about going to San Diego two days early on a work trip and spending the money on front-row seats at The War on Drugs concert. It's about lingering longer on the front porch to take in that sunset. It's about going to work late so I can play "just one more game" of croquet with my grandson. It's about investing in a good mountain bike because it gives me such life when I ride. It's about radically investing in others through Harbor Ministries in ways that make no sense.

It's about dreaming big, bringing Steve Ferrone, the drummer from Tom Petty and the Heartbreakers, to Lincoln, Nebraska, for a Tom Petty tribute night. Why? Simply because I love Tom Petty music. Many of his songs have brought depth into the leadership events we do with Harbor Ministries. And we thought it would be fun to give the Lincoln community a gift.

It's about going to Estes Park or San Diego almost ninety times in the last decade as we have invited leaders from around the country into a RHYTHMinTWENTY or ROGUE JOURNEY with Harbor. It is about keeping the tradition of fishing alive with my sons and hiking this summer to an upper-elevation tea house high in the Canadian Rockies with my daughter. Staying wild is all of this and so much more.

The world has been shaken; life seems different. People seem more fearful and filled with uncertainty. But the last thing the world needs is for you and I to settle in, play it safe, step back from the edge, and be insulated from others and the culture. The world and those around us need to see us steady, anchored, and solid, but still willing to step out. We need that as well. Our hearts, souls, and lives demand that we stay in a wild pursuit of life and of God.

This is your invitation away from safety and toward the edge—toward that place where I believe God will meet you and you will find life.

Let's journey toward the wild together. But before we go, we must learn to stay.

Tim Bohlke

# Part 1:
# Stay

## Chapter 1: Stay

In explaining why I wrote this book, I mentioned the wildfire near Estes Park in the fall of 2020. The East Troublesome fire burned nearly 194,000 acres and was the second-largest wildfire ever recorded in Colorado. Images from those days and the moments around that fire are seared into my mind.

One of those images was the drive on I-76 as we headed toward Denver and then on to Estes Park for a strategic gathering. For nearly 100 miles as we drove, we followed a funnel of clouds and dark smoke that we knew originated from the eastern slope of the Rockies. It was midday, yet the sun was blocked, and we had an ominous feeling as we drove closer to the source of that darkness. That feeling seemed to mirror the season of life both Bryan Olesen and I were in as we made that drive.

That evening, we sat in our favorite brewery having a beer. As we waited for others to arrive the next morning, there was this sense that something was off. Even though fire was burning near Grand Lake just forty-six miles away, there seemed to be little concern in Estes Park. No evacuations had been ordered, and the town seemed somewhat normal . . . except that as we talked, a steady stream of ashes fell out of the night sky into our beer. So much ash was falling that we had to move inside. It was a sign of things to come.

The fall of 2020 was a hard time for everyone as the world faced so much uncertainty in this crazy year of COVID. The leaders and pastors who would soon join us at Harbor's recently purchased anchor site, the Blue Spruce Manor, really needed to connect with God after such a weary season. And the truth was that Bryan and

I were going through a tough, challenging season in our own lives as well. It was a pretty dark time as I faced some newly discovered health challenges and wrestled with unresolved disappointment in God and others. So many of the leaders I talked to around the country and those meeting us the next day were so weary from the ongoing disruptions of a pandemic, politics, upheaval, chaos, noise. We all longed for and needed a reprieve, if only for a few days. The Blue Spruce Manor is the anchor site for all our events and a place where God has met many of us in significant ways. We were beaten down and desperately needed to connect with God and each other. We got a few hours of respite, then everything changed.

Late the next morning, the winds shifted, and the skies grew red. The fires closed in on Estes. We were on a short hike when we learned that a mandatory evacuation was ordered for the area. As we walked back to the Blue Spruce, we heard a loudspeaker from a nearby emergency vehicle saying, "Do not wait! Get in your vehicles and evacuate the area immediately."

*You've got to be kidding!*

My mind raced. We had only recently taken a risk and purchased this two-million-dollar property in Estes Park, and we were still more than a million dollars in debt. We hoped that once we paid off the property, it would not only house events but become a passive income producer to help fuel Harbor's mission going forward. We walked through the house, said our goodbyes, and jumped in our cars.

Soon we joined the mass exodus heading down the mountain. Then I saw him—this dude fly fishing in the river, as calm as could be. He was out of place, a paradox, and I was mesmerized. Not fifty yards from him, both sides of the highway were packed with cars escaping the encroaching flames. The smell of smoke hung thick in the air. The ashes that had been drifting into our beers the night before were now blowing in a more significant way.

Yet, amid all that was going on, that fisherman was in great rhythm casting his fly rod.

*Is he absolutely crazy?*

*Is he at all aware of what's going on here?*

Then, my assessment of the man's sanity was interrupted by an overwhelming thought: *Whatever he's got, I need!*

As we made our slow descent away from the raging fires, I watched him as long as I could. That, I realized, is exactly what I want Harbor Ministries to be. I want Harbor to be a space where people can be still in the eye of the storm. I want us to develop leaders who know how to find space, to get quiet, and to find strength and courage no matter what they face or what may be swirling around them. I hope that I, and the many we work with across the country, can be an anchor of sorts for others in disruptive times. I want them to know how to stay—and stay solid, grounded, unshaken —even when everything seems to be unraveling.

Now hear me: I'm not advocating for ignoring mandatory evacuation orders or not applying wisdom and common sense. But I have no doubt I was supposed to see and experience that moment. I needed to see that fisherman that day personally. As I process it a few years later, it is an image that has encouraged and inspired me to keep going, both in my own life and in leading this organization that is committed to helping, challenging, encouraging, and inspiring others to find game-changing rhythm and strength even in the worst of times.

So as you start the journey of this book, I am pleading with you to learn how to stay—how to remain, how to abide, how to be still—in the center of God's presence no matter your circumstances, no matter how shaken and disrupted the world seems around you.

## Be Still

One of God's crazy invitations to us is to be still. This phrase appears throughout scripture in some harrowing scenarios. In war, in chaos, in political turmoil, in drought, in uncertainty, in famine, in pain, He says, "Be still and know that I am God." In the following Psalm, the placement of the phrase makes no sense. It does not seem to fit the flow of this passage, Yet amid the utter chaos of this Psalm comes this single verse that screams, "Be still."

> God is our refuge and strength, an ever-present help in trouble.
>
> Therefore we will not fear, though the earth give way and the mountains fall into the sea, though the waters roar and foam and the mountains quake with their surging.
>
> There is a river whose streams make glad the city of God, the holy place where the Most High dwells.
>
> God is within her, she will not fail:
>
> God will help her at break of day.
>
> Nations are in uproar, kingdoms fall;
>
> He lifts his voice, the earth melts
>
> The Lord Almighty is with us; the God of Jacob is our fortress.
>
> Come and see what the Lord has done, the desolations he has brought on earth.
>
> He makes wars cease to the ends of the earth.
>
> He breaks the bow and shatters the spear; he burns the shields with fire.
>
> He says, 'Be still, and know that I am God; I will be exalted among the nations,

I will be exalted in the earth.'

The Lord Almighty is with us;

The God of Jacob is our fortress.

(Psalm 46, NIV)

Let's take God up on his invitation. Let's be still and sit with this. Our default is to rush through our to-do list, to move from activity to task, from task to activity. Let's break that cycle now. Let's rest in God's invitation. Your goal is not to finish reading this page or chapter. Your purpose for the moment is to quiet your mind, to settle your heart. Take a deep breath and listen. Hear what God is saying.

*Be still.*

*Be.*

*Still.*

*In all this craziness in the news . . . in the world . . . in the country . . . in your own life . . .*

*be still.*

*In this moment of stillness and quiet, you can know that I am God.*

*You can know.*

*I am God.*

*I will be honored by every nation.*

*I will be honored throughout the world.*

*The Lord of Heaven's Armies is right here. The God of Israel.*

*I am your fortress.*

Stay here.

Linger.

Remain.

Sit with the words that God is speaking over you.

Quiet your thoughts.

Listen.

See, when we're still, that's when strength and courage can come. That's when clarity can come. When we're still, we can be reminded that God is our fortress. We can be reminded that the angel armies sit right here with us wherever we are. Ready. Denying. Defending. Detecting.

When we are still, we can be assured that He can stop wars. He can break the bow. He can cause conflicts to end. He can make the mountains tremble and the oceans roar. And our circumstances don't matter so much because He is right here with us. His voice thunders and the earth melts.

When we are still, we're reminded that we aren't alone. Not only do we have our Father's steadfast, steadying presence, but we also discover He has given us guides to help us through these murky waters. We can't do this alone. We need others. God invites us to be attentive. To look for guides who are a few steps or miles ahead of us on the journey. To learn from them and, at times, to follow their footsteps along the path. To draw from their courage to forge a new way when God leads.

Tom Osborne was a football coach at Nebraska. He won nine or more games in each of his twenty-five seasons and claimed three national championships. His presence and influence in Nebraska are significant. Now I've been a huge college football fan my whole life, but the moment that had the biggest impact on me was not when Osborne was a coach but rather a congressman. Congressman Osborne appeared in a video shown at Nebraska's Memorial Stadium in September of 2001. Nebraska was playing the first football game in America after the 9/11 attacks. I took my kids to the game, and I'll never forget the mix of excitement, hesitation, and even guarded fear in the stadium that night. Just before kickoff, Osborne was on the big screen from his office in Washington, DC. His last words were, "We are going to be okay." A collective sigh spread through the 80,000 in attendance. We needed someone we respected to assure us, give us a sense of hope, and remind us of the big picture. In that moment, I saw the power of respected leadership. It doesn't take much: a life where words and action align, a genuine care for people, and a willingness to enter into the difficult critical moments.

As I consider the difference-making people I've known, age and vocation have not been factors. I wonder what gives their lives such weight and strength. How did they seem to stay steady and be such anchors in turbulent times? My dad was one of those difference-makers. He died when he was only fifty-nine. That seemed young then, even more so as I process it today. He has been gone for more than thirty years, but I still hear stories about how he impacted others. A farmer in Central Nebraska. A guy who taught a Sunday school class for decades. A man who seemed to provide stability and steadiness to everyone who knew him, even in the most difficult times. At his funeral, I probably had six men come up to me and tell me they had lost their best friend that day. So what was it about him?

I was only twenty-six when my dad died. I have lived many more years without him than I had with him. I remember so many things about Dad, but one of the enduring images is of him at the end of each day when he would take long, quiet walks. I can remember as a teenager, watching him take these walks and, in his own way, talk with God. I believe those regular walks prepared him for both the good times and the hard times. His practice of connecting with

God in his own way, at his pace, was one thing that separated him.

So let's let my dad guide us. Let's follow his footsteps. Let's walk slowly through the last part of Psalm 46. Read the following words several times using the guide below.

> Come, see the glorious works of the Lord: See how he brings destruction upon the world.
>
> He causes wars to end throughout the earth. He breaks the bow and snaps the spear; he burns the shields with fire.
>
> 'Be still and know that I am God! I will be honored by every nation. I will be honored throughout the world.'
>
> The Lord of Heaven's Armies is here Among us; the God of Israel is our fortress.
>
> (Psalm 46:8-11, NLT)

As you read the passage again, be mindful of what is stirring in your mind and spirit. What words and phrases are rising to the surface? Hold on to them.

> Come, see the glorious works of the Lord:
>
> See how he brings destruction upon the world.
>
> He causes wars to end throughout the earth.
>
> He breaks the bow and snaps the spear; he burns the shields with fire.
>
> Be still and know that I am God!
>
> I will be honored by every nation. I will be honored throughout the world.
>
> The Lord of Heaven's Armies is here Among us; the God of

Israel is our fortress.

Go ahead and speak out a word, a phrase that God has given you.

This passage is chaotic, the setting intense. The storms are surging. Mountains are crumbling into the sea. The earth is shaken. Then it talks about God as a warrior. He can ban wars from pole to pole and break the weapons across his knee. I mean, he can stop the conflicts that are going on right now when he chooses. But in the midst of all this crazy comes one of the most famous verses in all of the Bible:

Be still.

Be still and know that I am God!

It doesn't seem to fit, yet there it is, right in the middle of this intense passage. Why? I think it's because out of stillness comes strength. Out of stillness comes perspective. Out of stillness, we find the time to remember the ways God has shown up in our lives. Out of stillness comes the kind of strength and resolve that can inspire others. The kind I saw in my dad.

I'm drawn back to the image of the guy fly fishing as we evacuated fires near Estes Park in the fall of 2020. And again, I long for that ability to be so still and so focused in the middle of chaos. So let's go back to Psalm 46 once more from a different translation. Let's soak in God's word one more time.

> Attention, all! See the marvels of God! He plants flowers and trees all over the earth,
> Bans wars from pole to pole, breaks the weapons across his knee.
> 'Step out of the traffic! Take a long, loving look at me, your High God, above politics, above everything.'
> Jacob-wrestling God fights for us, God-of-Angel-Armies protects us.
> (Psalm 46:8-11, MSG)

Carry the words with you and go outside for a long, slow walk.

## Chapter 2: Stay in The Moment

When anxiety and fear are running high, there's a good chance we are worried about the future or obsessing over the past. We can't change or control either of those things. One thing that helps us stay grounded is learning to be fully in the present moment.

Now I'm a visionary, so I'm always thinking ahead. It's where my mind automatically goes, and there is great value in vision and planning. But many times when I am looking forward, I'm missing the moments right now.

I don't know how many of you saw the 2020 Michael Jordan documentary, *The Last Dance.* We all remember that very long spring. The world was closing down. They had canceled the NCAA basketball tournament and the NBA season. Everything was changing. Nothing felt normal. We all wondered if things would ever be the same again. It felt desolate. As a fan, I craved anything sports related to help me escape for a few hours, and there was nothing. Then came *The Last Dance.* What an incredible gift in that moment. I know it's strange, but watching the story of Michael Jordan's career felt right, even comforting. Truthfully, when I think back to that time, that documentary really helped me. It connected me to the fun and great moments and memories of basketball and all the life circumstances surrounding those moments. It reminded me of a time when life felt normal.

As a basketball fan, I appreciated the story of victory, loss, accomplishments, drivenness, success, failures, excitement, and disappointment. I loved it! At the beginning of the last episode, they talked about one thing that made Michael unique, one thing that separated him from others, and it was not what you might think. The Chicago Bulls were heading into the 1998 NBA finals against the Utah Jazz. If the Bulls could beat their archrivals, it would be an incredible six championships for Jordan and his team. One of the men traveling with the Bulls said that Michael had an innate ability to be fully in the moment, to be fully present. He did not let past failures define him; he did not live in what ifs. He was never anywhere else.

Jordan spent his whole life prepping for greatness with a lot of vision and movement toward what could be, and the thought of winning another NBA championship always drove him. But when the ball tipped, he was fully present in the game. He was able to cut out the distractions, shut off the noise, and be right there. He identified that ability to be fully engaged in the moment as the difference-maker that separated him from the other elite athletes who played in the NBA.

Matthew 6 can help us get there. I remember being at a middle school church camp decades ago when I first heard this passage. Somehow, even then, these concepts seemed profound: stop worrying and asking questions that have no solid answers. Seek him first, and the rest will take care of itself.

> So do not worry, saying, 'What shall we eat?' or 'What shall we drink?' or 'What shall we wear?'
>
> For the pagans run after all these things and your heavenly Father knows that you need them.
>
> But seek first his kingdom and his righteousness, and all these things will be given to you as well.
>
> Therefore do not worry about tomorrow, for tomorrow will worry about itself.

> Each day has enough trouble of its own.
>
> (Matthew 6:31-34, NIV)

Let's let the reality of those words soak in. The creator of the universe, the God who gave everything so we could have this moment with him, tells us not to worry. He's got this. He's got us.

Reread the passage. It's a great challenge. "Seek first . . . and all these things will be given unto you as well. So don't worry about tomorrow, for tomorrow will worry about itself."

What word or phrase can you hold onto today?

When he was young, our older son had a remarkable ability to help us stay right in the moment with him. If he sensed I was distracted when he was talking to me, he'd come up and kind of grab my face and hold it in front of him so he knew I was listening and focused on him. That gesture was such a clear visual of what it meant to stay in the moment.

This is part of what Matthew 6 is trying to tell us. Shut down the distractions, unplug from the noise. Focus on the present moment. There's a lot to think about for tomorrow; its time will come. There's a lot to wonder about and learn from yesterday, but we can't miss what God is doing here right now.

Staying in the moment can be the difference-maker. It can be a separator.

## Chapter 3: Navigating the *Midbar*

What comes to mind when you hear the word wilderness?

Lost?

Barren?

Lonely?

Foreboding?

Severe?

Struggle?

When we describe our struggles, loss, conflicts, and pain, we often refer to it as going through the wilderness. But what if the wilderness is also a holy place, a place of clarity and strength? A place—maybe the main place—where we can hear God?

Jesus starts his whole ministry journey with forty days in the wilderness. After thirty years of waiting, John baptizes Jesus in the Jordan. Finally, after thirty years, Jesus steps out of the shadows and is ready to walk onto the public stage. But what's the first thing he does? He heads to the wilderness by himself for forty days. When we think of this part of Jesus's story, we often think about it as the enemy wearing Jesus down, trying to tempt him while he's in a frail, weakened state. But what if it's something entirely different? What if the wilderness was a place of strengthening that readied Jesus for the next three years?

Philosopher and theologian Dallas Willard wrote, "The place of solitude and deprivation, was actually the place of strengthening for our Lord, the Spirit led him there . . . to ensure that Christ was in the best possible condition for the trial. In the desert solitude, Jesus fasted for more than a month. Then, and not before, Satan was allowed to approach him with his glittering proposals of bread, notoriety, and power. Only then was Jesus at the height of his strength. The desert was his fortress, his place of power. Throughout his life he sought the solitary place as an indirect submission of his own physical body to righteousness (ie Mark 1:35; 3:13; 6:31,46). That is, he sought it not as an activity done for its own sake, but one done to give him power for good." [1]

Jesus's followers knew of his practice of seeking solitude and imitated it in the centuries after his death.

The Hebrew word for wilderness is ***midbar***. ***Midbar*** comes from the root word ***davar***, which means to speak. So what if it is, in fact, the wilderness—the places of struggle—where God truly breaks through? Can we come to see the wilderness as a place of strengthening, a place where we can hear God's voice more clearly than at any other time in our lives?

I know this has been the case in my journey. A few months ago, I was in San Diego getting ready for two different leadership events we do with the organization I lead, Harbor Ministries. Over a decade into this journey, we have brought more than thirty groups to San Diego and more than fifty groups to Colorado. I was coming into this season tired and weary. I was unsure I had what it would take to continue bringing the passion, focus, and intensity these leaders deserved. So there I sat for hours above the cliffs in La Jolla, watching the waves come in, asking God if I still have what it takes.

> Journal Entry, June 16, 2022
>
> *I feel pretty spent emotionally and spiritually. Do I have enough left in the tank to keep doing this? It's an interesting season in life. Harbor is going well . . . funding is currently strong, impact is at an all-time high . . . but I feel worn from this fast and intensive pace we have been on. How long can I keep this pace?*

The longer I sat, the more I had this sense I needed to keep going.

> *Just like these waves, you keep coming, keep taking the next step. I'll give you the energy and passion you need in the moment.*

As I sat there, I was drawn to the story of Moses. Out of that struggle, as I wondered if my time leading Harbor needed to enter a different season, came the words, the imagery, and the steady strength to keep going.

Did Moses also find the wilderness a place of strength? He is in the wilderness, tending sheep, running his father-in-law's business.

He's been at this for forty years. This is Moses! Moses, who was given up by his mom and taken into Pharaoh's family and a life of privilege. As an adult, he discovers he's the son of Hebrew slaves. When he sees an Egyptian master mistreat a Hebrew slave, he snaps. As a result, Moses is banished to the wilderness.

Now, it's forty years in. Moses is around the age of eighty. He's likely settled in, thinking this is how his life will play out, every day like the one before. And he had to be thinking this isn't a bad gig: run the father-in-law's business, take the sheep up the mountain, keep them fed and safe, and do it again the next day. We pick up the story on a day Moses likely thought was another ordinary day, just another day among the 14,600 other days in that desert wilderness. That's what makes this story so amazing and so relatable. This first simple, radical, relational, crazy encounter we hear about between Moses and God comes after four decades of desert time.

> Now Moses was pasturing the flock of his father-in-law Jethro, the priest of Midian; and he led the flock to the west side of the wilderness and came to Horeb, the mountain of God. The angel of the Lord appeared to him in a blazing fire from the midst of a bush; and he looked, and behold, the bush was burning with fire, yet the bush was not consumed. So Moses said, 'I must turn aside now and see this marvelous sight, why the bush is not burned up!' When the Lord saw that he turned aside to look, God called to him from the midst of the bush and said, 'Moses, Moses!'
>
> . . . And the Lord said, 'I have surely seen the affliction of My people who are in Egypt and have heard their outcry because of their taskmasters, for I am aware of their sufferings.

So I have come down to rescue them from the power of the Egyptians, and to bring them up from that land to a good and spacious land, to a land flowing with milk and honey . . .

And now, behold, the cry of the sons of Israel has come to Me; furthermore, I have seen the oppression with which the Egyptians are oppressing them.

And now come, and I will send you to Pharaoh, so that you may bring My people, the sons of Israel, out of Egypt.'

(Portions of Exodus 3:1-10, NASB)

Two things catch my attention. First, God does speak. Second, Moses doesn't miss it. He pauses. He turns aside. He notices when God shows up. Can you recall a time when you didn't slow down or pause? Are you moving so fast, running to keep up, pressing on with the urgent, that you might miss the burning bush in your backyard? Let's not rush through this passage.

This dramatic story raises many difficult questions. The Hebrew people had been suffering under slavery for generations. For hundreds of years! Why did God wait so long to show up? And even if Moses was the man for the job, why wait another forty years before giving him this mission? Perhaps part of the reason it took forty years was that Moses was not ready. He was not listening. Only when God saw Moses turn aside did he speak. Verse four tells us that when God saw Moses turn aside, ***then*** he spoke. Let that sink in for a moment. I believe this is one of the most dramatic moments in the Bible. Had Moses walked by the burning bush before? I recently read that the crystal in the sand in that desert can actually cause a fire when the conditions are right. Over the years, Moses may actually have seen many a bush explode into flame.

But this time is different; the bush does not burn up, and Moses is going slow enough that he notices. God waits until Moses is ready, until he pays attention.

When Moses pauses, when he notices, when he listens, God speaks clearly, but he doesn't tell Moses specifics. He basically says, "So you, yes you, just one guy, go into the most powerful country on earth and lead a million people out of slavery." Well, those weren't his exact words.

> 'And now come, and I will send you to Pharaoh, so that you may bring My people, the sons of Israel, out of Egypt.' But Moses said to God, 'Who am I, that I should go to Pharaoh, and that I should bring the sons of Israel out of Egypt?' And He said, 'Assuredly I will be with you . . .'
>
> (Exodus 3:10-12, NASB)

God does not give Moses a plan but a promise: I will be with you. I've often wondered why the Hebrews were willing to follow Moses, but I think the answer is pretty simple: They followed Moses because he had met God. He not only met with God in this encounter in Exodus, but he would meet with him many times over the next forty years. He met with God and he stayed in those moments as long as it took.

If we want to lead, if we want to take risks and move beyond the boundaries to do the wild things that God is calling us to, we must first make it a practice to meet God. It needs to be a mark of our lives. We simply must be willing to go into the wilderness, endure times of struggle, loneliness, and pain, and bear the dry seasons when life seems mundane, even pointless. Time and again in my life, these are the spaces where God breaks through.

So let me finish the story. As I sat by the ocean, tired and ready to give up, I wrote these words in my journal:

> June 16, 2022
>
> *. . . waves kept coming, and the message for me seems to be I need to keep coming as well. Like these waves' relentless motion, I just need to take the next step, keep bringing my best into these moments, and he will give me the words I need, the passion, and the strength I need to do this well. I was drawn to the words in Isaiah 58:10–13, and I read them again and again.* 'I will always show you where to go. I'll give you a full life in the emptiest of places . . . you will be like a well-watered garden, a gurgling spring that never runs dry. . . . You'll be known as those who can fix anything, restore old ruins, rebuild and renovate . . .' (Isaiah 58:10-13, MSG)
>
> *I felt like this could be true of me if I could just keep going, but the real gift is in verse eleven:* 'Feed the hungry, and help those in trouble. Then your light will shine . . . The Lord will guide you continually, giving you water when you are dry . . . ' (Isaiah 58:10-11, NLT)

In this moment, God met me and gave me what I needed. I came out of that time not immediately energized but ready to take the next step and keep swinging. And as each day passed as I led these groups, I gained more focus, resolve, and energy for the mission.

With so much vying for our attention, how do we not miss it? How do we make sure we turn aside and don't walk right past the burning bush? How do we keep taking that next step, just like those relentless waves that keep coming? How do we get ourselves in a place to trust those words, "He will give you water when you are dry"?

## Stay Attentive

I'm pretty sure I have some form of attention deficit disorder. My mind is so often racing to the next thing, so staying focused, listening, and paying attention can be a struggle. Yet I don't want to walk by the burning bush. I want to find a place to stand at attention and really listen. I believe that in every season of wilderness—even the wilderness you may find yourself in now—there is this place, a moment where a life-changing encounter awaits us. It's critical that we be attentive so we don't miss it.

I love to hike a trail above Crested Butte, Colorado. It's a place I return to often. The trail starts above Schofield Pass, and if you follow its entire length, it will take you twelve miles across the wilderness, past the Maroon Bells, and into Aspen, Colorado. But a few miles up this trail, you can get to the top of Schofield Mountain. As a more "seasoned" flatlander, I always feel good about myself if I make it up this mountain. The last part of the climb is a rugged trek on loose rock. At times, you are on all fours. The rough route to the top can get crazy, but as you take the last steps up this rock field that seems to last forever, you find an incredible reward. You come to a small patch of grassy meadow that really doesn't belong there but invites you to rest and take in the view.

Over the years, I have spent hours sitting in the meadow. I have journaled. I have sat in quiet awe. I have lamented as I dealt with disappointments and struggles. I have wrestled with God there. I lost both of my parents before I was thirty-five, and I had had it with God. I was ready to be done. I had too many questions, and he seemed so detached. Distant. Silent. But somehow, he met me in that small meadow in the middle of a thousand feet of rock and shale. That meadow was an unexpected, unplanned place of refuge. And through decades of leadership—amazing seasons and some intensely dark, difficult times—there were always those moments . . .

this place . . .

this meadow . . .

where he met me.

This place in the desolate wilderness where I can hear his voice.

I have had to learn to be attentive. I must fight for the time to still myself. In Harbor, we call this practice SPACE. It's so vital it is one of the first things we challenge leaders to make a priority. We model taking regular, extended times to step away, shut off the noise, and tune all our senses to the one who so often whispers in a still, small voice.

How does taking SPACE become a habit? A discipline? Start from where you are. Try it for one hour. Not someday, but today. Shut off your phone. Get away from your usual surroundings. Get outside if possible.

Begin by being still and quiet.

Ask God to remind you of times he has broken through during hard seasons in your life. Write about those moments. Reflect on how your life has changed because of them.

Read the story of Moses from Exodus 3:1-10. Pause and listen. Ask God what he wants to say.

Reread the passage. Journal about any words or phrases that stand out.

Read the passage slowly a third time. Invite God to interrupt your routine. If you've been walking past the burning bush or been too busy or distracted to turn aside, ask for his forgiveness. Ask God to hone your attentiveness and alert you to his presence.

Don't stop. Now that you've tasted SPACE, try it for more extended periods of time. See our radical invitation in chapter six to take an entire day each month to be still and quiet with God.

Can we begin to see the wilderness seasons of our journeys with new eyes? The wilderness is not only a place of pain, desperation, and isolation but a place where the distractions are stripped away, and we can hear God more clearly.

Brad Brestel is a friend and pastor who was part of a ROGUE JOURNEY group that started in 2013. He had no idea that he was about to enter the wilderness. The message he heard from God on his first Rogue trip seemed anticlimactic: *Don't start anything new. Steady the course.*

A trip to his dentist in August 2013 was the first indication something was wrong. An oral surgeon and ENT doctor found a tumor at the back of Brad's tongue, but the initial biopsy indicated it was benign. Out-patient surgery to remove the annoying mass was scheduled for the end of September. Brad planned to be at the surgery center for four or five hours. Instead, he woke up in a hospital room where he learned he had cancer. He spent the next five months undergoing radiation and chemo treatments and enduring unbearable pain in his mouth and throat. Even water burned to swallow. At one point, they thought they might have to remove Brad's tongue. He had weeks when he couldn't talk, and when his voice returned, it was weak and quiet. It was a lonely, scary time.

But God had prepared Brad for this desert. Brad had already settled the question of whether God is good. As he describes it,

The question was answered by his lead pastor in a sermon when he said, "I walked that dog a long time ago."

"I liked that statement, and right there, I decided that God was good," Brad recalls. And even when he was in excruciating pain with his face clamped down during radiation, his feet were "super glued to the rock and never slipped."

And God met Brad in that year of pain and quiet. At the end of the time, he told his ROGUE cohorts that he had learned he is mortal and can't waste the time God has given him. He also has a better understanding of pain and more compassion for those who experience unrelenting suffering. And he learned how materialistic he is.

"Before cancer I was busy adding to the collection of stuff, and using gobs of time to operate, clean, maintain, and spending money to insure all that stuff. I was spending way too much time with stuff, and not nearly enough time with people and God. It's hard to love God and people when you would rather be with your stuff. I repent. I was blind. I am so glad ROGUE prepared me for a long season of silence, and a time I could really hear God."

Jewish Messianic Rabbi and author Jonathan Cahn echoes Brad's words:

> "So God brings us into the wilderness that we might actually hear his voice. Don't fear the wilderness, don't despise his removing of distractions . . . embrace it, draw close to him and listen, seek to hear his voice, and you will hear him. The wilderness in your life is not just wilderness it is Holy ground. it is *midbar* the place he speaks, the place of HIS voice."[2]
>
> -Johnathan Cahn

## Chapter 4: Stay Aware

So often in my life, and I suspect in yours too, it's taken a crisis or moments of struggle or pain to get my attention, awaken me and cause me to seek God. Several years ago, my son, a gifted athlete, was on track to have a Division 1 college basketball scholarship. Man, it was the ride of our lives! So much fun. But as he entered his senior year, a rash of injuries started. At the height of his success and in the frenzy of recruiting, the first injury hit, and you could tell it was something significant. Four months through that stretch, I remember praying every day that God would take that injury from my son and give it to me. I poured out all kinds of prayers. Heal him. Touch him. Help him be who you created him to be. Bring him back to a place where he can use the gifts you have given him. He would use this influence through athletics to impact so many others. Let him do it. Clear this obstacle. I sounded a little like Asaph, the man who wrote several of the Psalms I am so drawn to. Asaph was honest and wore his emotions on his sleeve.

Or there is David. On the heels of personal failure at one of the darkest moments in his life, he wrote Psalm 51. He had an affair that set off a chain of events that would change everything in his life, his family, and his leadership. As David writes, he pleads for a way out of the darkness in his soul. Through his words, he gives us a pathway to how we can encounter God, no matter the circumstances of life.

> Create in me a clean heart, God, And renew a steadfast spirit within me.
>
> Do not cast me away from Your presence. And do not take Your Holy Spirit from me.

> Restore to me the joy of Your salvation, And sustain me with a willing spirit.
>
> *Then* I will teach wrongdoers Your ways, And sinners will be converted to You.
>
> (Psalm 51:10-13, NASB)

As is our practice, let's pause and read these verses again. This time, make these words your prayer. I believe God will meet you there.

> Create in me a clean heart, God, And renew a steadfast spirit within me.
>
> Do not cast me away from Your presence. And do not take Your Holy Spirit from me.
>
> Restore to me the joy of Your salvation, And sustain me with a willing spirit.
>
> *Then* I will teach wrongdoers Your ways, And sinners will be converted to You.
>
> (Psalm 51:10-13, NASB)

Verse twelve feels like the key to me. "Restore to me the joy of Your salvation and sustain me with a willing spirit," and ***then*** things will happen. The invitation in David's words is to remember—remember when God showed up and restored some joy. The key to being aware and alert to what God is doing today is remembering what he has done in the past.

Do you remember that first moment God became real—when he entered your story and became really real? For me, it was the last couple of years in college. In those first years, I went a little crazy and crossed a lot of lines. As I came out of the season determined to make up for lost time, I was willing to do anything, go anywhere, talk to anyone, and follow God no matter what. There simply was no obstacle that would stop me, and I was willing to risk a lot. It seemed like nothing would slow me down. Eventually, life happened, but there was such passion and joy in the beginning! To be able to think back and reflect on those early days of walking with God, when I was driven by both my head and heart, changes my perspective and helps me refocus. Remember.

So how about you? How has God shown up in the last day or week or year? How has his story intersected yours? Do you remember those moments? Where were you? Who were you with? What were you doing, or what did you see or experience? Don't forget them. Write them down. Remind yourself of times you were stirred or you felt movement when you had been stuck. Maybe it was triggered by something as simple as the words of a song, a scene in a movie, that amazing sunset, or an inspiring conversation.

Psalm 105 speaks to this. There is such gold in this passage. I really think it has something important for you.

> Hallelujah!
>
> Thank God! Pray to him by name! Tell everyone you meet what he has done!
>
> Sing him songs, belt out hymns, translate his wonders to music!
>
> Honor his holy name with Hallelujahs, you who seek God. Live a happy life!
>
> Keep your eyes open for God, *watch* for his works; be *alert* for signs of his presence.

*Remember* the world of wonders he has made.

(Psalm 105:1-6a, MSG, Emphasis ours)

It's right there in the middle of the Bible, the key to staying grounded in our faith: "Keep your eyes open for God. Watch for his works, be alert to the signs of his presence. Remember the world of Wonders."

These moments of remembering, of awareness that God is present and moving, often come at random times. A line from a song or a scene from a movie will hit me differently if I'm locked in and paying attention. I was listening to the radio this morning when "The Cave" by Mumford and Sons began to play, and the words resonated. I remembered who God has promised to be and how he has grounded me, held me, and still calls my name.

I recently saw *The Jesus Revolution*. In one scene, a pastor who has been stuck in his ways in a lifeless place is suddenly awakened by the words of a hippie who challenges him not to forget that God's heart is reaching out to everyone. Maybe it's time he and his congregation feel some discomfort and remember that God welcomes everyone—I mean everyone and anyone, no matter what they have done or are doing, no matter what has been done to them. It doesn't matter; the door is open. This simple, profound moment becomes a catalyst for a movement.

Way back when I was at middle school church camp, the words of a song started me on a spiritual journey that I'm still on today. I remember how I felt as we sang, "Turn your eyes upon Jesus." As an eighth grader, I remember thinking life really does feel different; other things don't seem as important. Other things fade in comparison to what that moment at camp felt like. It was the first of many reminders over the years that we just get glimpses, moments that remind us that something greater is coming, something that won't be gone so quickly. Renewal and restoration of how this life is supposed to be are coming.

Another glimpse came a few months ago when I was twenty feet from Marcus Mumford as he sang "Awake My Soul." My heart needed those words so badly at that moment. I also experienced an unsettling, kind of scary, awe-inspiring moment sitting near an active volcano in Iceland. Along with the sheer power of the volcano was the peace that God's got this. It is his voice that thunders and melts the earth.

Many years ago, I dropped our youngest son off at a friend's house for a play date. As I left, I felt a strong urge to turn around and go back. When I reached the backyard, I saw five-year-old Dylan neck-deep in their pond. Instead of walking around to where the kids were playing, he decided to take the more direct route straight across the water. What if I hadn't been aware of God's nudge in that moment? What if I'd been distracted, thinking about getting to the next thing on my schedule?

God shows up, often in ordinary moments that can be extraordinary if we're attentive to them. Are we alert? Listening? Are we ready to act, to turn aside if needed? Will we pause long enough to notice?

## Chapter 5: Stay Anchored

Clouds will form

Winds will blow

The waves will try to drown my hope

Oh the darkness will fall

The waters will rise

But my anchor will hold through the night.

-Bryan Olesen, "Jesus Be My Harbor"

As I write this in 2023, the world as we know it has been shaken. Countries, leaders, politics, religion, people's lives, the way we think, and how we process have been disrupted. I have never been through an earthquake, but I'm told it can shake you to the core, and the experience tends to change your perspective. What you once assumed was solid now appears vulnerable. You live in the unknown, unsure when another quake or aftershock might rock your world again. In fact, it is the frequent aftershocks that bring so much fear and uncertainty. That is how it feels coming out of the pandemic. The world seems upside down, shaken, disoriented, and unlikely to return to normal, whatever normal means.

While on a recent trip to Central Florida, I got a text from my wife.

*Call me right away.*

Nothing else. No details. I was in the middle of a sweet time, attending events with people impacted by Harbor Ministries. The connections, the music, and the relationships were filling my tanks until that text. My gut turned. It was like a trigger. Fear took over. Memories of hard things with our kids, loss, and disappointment flooded my mind.

*What is it this time?*

It was a water purifier. In my wild imaginings of what was happening at home, the water purifier never crossed my mind. The text immediately sent me to worst-case scenarios as if I was programmed. Had the many hard things we had gone through as a family conditioned me that much to expect bad news? Had three years of COVID-19 left me in a perpetual state of anxiety with this feeling that the next shoe was about to drop? Really nothing feels stable, does it? Finances, the stock market, housing, world events, the wars and conflicts that never seem to stop, and the heartbreak we see continually playing out in so many parts of the world. Life and how I respond to it has changed.

When the world shut down in 2020 and everything felt shaky, I needed something to hold on to. Psalm 62 became significant to me. It was something solid, something that provided staying power.

> My soul, wait in silence for God alone, For my hope is from Him.
>
> He alone is my rock and my salvation, My refuge; I will not be shaken
>
> My salvation and my glory rest on God; The rock of my strength, my refuge is in God.
>
> Trust in Him at all times, you people;
>
> Pour out your hearts before Him;
>
> God is a refuge for us.
>
> (Psalm 62:5-9, NASB)

We need these words more than ever. We don't have to be greatly shaken. There is a way to keep our feet on solid ground, no matter what the world around us is doing. Spend some time with these words. Marinate in them. You know the rhythm. Read the passage three times. Pause in between. Focus on the words and phrases that resonate. Let God tend to your soul.

In these times of uncertainty, chaos, and struggle, we must continually remind ourselves that God is somehow in the mix of it all. None of this is surprising to him, and he can use all of it to bring people to himself. As I was thinking about writing this section today, I was drawn back to Psalm 46. One of the practices that keeps me anchored—not stagnant or dead in the water but connected to that which holds steady during the storm—is to return again and again to those places and things that bring me life. I do that with frequent rides on my bike, sometimes with scripture passages like Psalm 46, and by returning to places like the trail above Crested Butte.

I needed Psalm 46 again this morning, and I believe you need it, too. Those we influence and our families need these words, and we need the strength and the courage that can come as we settle into them. My hope is that we would believe that God is in the middle of our circumstances. Right here. Right now.

God is our refuge and strength, always ready to help in times of trouble. So we will not fear when earthquakes come and the mountains crumble into the sea. Let the oceans roar and foam. Let the mountains tremble as the waters surge!

A river brings joy to the city of our God, the sacred home of the Most High. God dwells in that city; it cannot be destroyed. From the very break of day, God will protect it. The nations are in chaos, and their kingdoms crumble! God's voice thunders, and the earth melts!

The Lord of Heaven's Armies is here among us; the God of Israel is our fortress.

(Psalm 46:1-7, NLT)

These aren't just some words of poetry. This isn't a story. These are words from the living, breathing God for us here in this season. So much chaos, so much uncertainty, and so many struggling with fear of the future. It's worth reading again.

> God is our refuge and strength, always ready to help in times of trouble.
>
> So we will not fear when the earthquakes come and the mountains crumble into the sea. Let the oceans roar and foam. Let the mountains tremble as the waters surge! A river brings joy to the city of our God, the sacred home of the Most High. God dwells in that city; it cannot be destroyed. From the very break of day, God will protect it.
>
> The nations are in chaos, and their kingdoms crumble! God's voice thunders and the earth melts! The Lord of Heaven's Armies is here among us; the God of Israel is our fortress.
>
> (Psalm 46:1-7, NLT)

When we find ourselves wrestling with fear, anxious about what will happen next, remember that God's voice thunders and the earth melts. We can find stability and strength amid this kind of chaos. I know we can. I've found it myself over the years and I have walked through it with others.

Heaven's armies are right here among us right now. They are with us wherever we're at in our story. And God is our rock-solid fortress. It's not that he can be a fortress, but that he is a fortress during the storms of life.

Now that is something solid. That gives us staying power in the days ahead.

## Chapter 6: Stay Quiet

In *The Comfort Crisis*, author Michael Easter reports that there are only twelve places in the lower forty-eight states where a person can sit in silence for thirty minutes or more and hear no man-made sounds. ***Only twelve places of absolute silence!*** That was incredible to me. There is truth to the idea that we are drowning in noise. Constant noise is damaging our bodies, our minds, and our spirits.

Several years Harbor Ministries took out a very expensive two-page ad in a national magazine. We hoped to create interest and generate new applications for our leadership journeys. There are always risks with advertising. The ad was costly, but the real risk was our approach—two empty white pages. On one side, in small print, we asked a simple question: Are you tired of the noise? Our URL appeared in the corner.

That was it. We paid thousands of dollars for white space, for a break from the noise of all the other ads screaming for attention. The magazine readily took our money but openly wondered how this could work. On more than one occasion, I asked the same questions. Are we crazy? Are we foolish to put so much into this ad? Why would anyone respond to this, let alone apply and commit to a two-year leadership journey?

The ad blew up and created a ton of interest and many applications. It hit on something significant: we long to figure out how to escape the noise. We must step away from all the noise; in fact, our emotional, spiritual, and physical health depends on it.

One of the men who saw that ad felt compelled to apply, but not immediately. He knew something was there for him, but too much was going on in his life. It wasn't until seven years later that he applied for Harbor's ROGUE leadership journey. He held onto that ad for seven years! He jumped into the ROGUE experience, not knowing anyone who had been through it. He wasn't sure what it was, but he knew he finally needed to respond. After all those years, only that ad and what it represented nudged him to take that radical step.

*In Comfort Crisis*, Easter notes that the world's number one killer is heart disease, but heart disease "is not just a consequence of too much couch and carbs. The World Health Organization found that the constant stream of decibels we live in is quite literally taking years off our lives."[3] So this idea of entering into silence is not only a pathway to God, it's a pathway to a longer life. It's more than a rhythm to life but a rhythm that will allow us to be more fully alive, alert, and wild going forward. Finding a day of silence, of SPACE, as our organization calls it, is an absolutely essential tool for living in a disrupted world.

More than fifteen years ago, I got a random call asking me to go to Quito, Ecuador, to speak at a leadership conference. The topic? What it looks like for a leader to stay the course and finish well. At that moment, I could not have felt less qualified. I was struggling in my faith, coming off a season where a perfect storm of fatigue, boredom, and disappointment was leading me to some dangerous and costly decisions. But thanks to the prodding of my wife and a sense from God that I could not bury, I went.

In the quiet on a mountain above Quito, Ecuador, God began to renew my vision of investing in emerging leaders. He stirred and awakened a dream, fueled my hope, and assured me it was time to use my voice to make a difference. On the heels of stepping out and speaking at that event in Ecuador, I knew it was time to launch this harbor—a place where weary leaders could come for hope, inspiration and encouragement, a place they could be challenged to live with life-changing rhythm, leave a legacy, and finish well. God also reminded me there would be costs: being on the front lines again of spiritual warfare, fundraising, relational and professional risks. Arrows and opposition would certainly come.

But in the time of extended quiet and solitude—a quiet that has become a vital rhythm in my life—I again felt my passion for pursuing God renewed. Through the years, getting these times alone with God has always, ***always*** been worth the fight.

I believe we can find renewal when we dare to practice seeking God in extended times of quiet. But I am hesitant to invite you to pursue God in this kind of space. These extended times of solitude can have a few minefields. In the last few years, these quiet times of listening have been dangerous for me. In the quiet, God has convicted me of things that should be changed, relationships I needed to let go of, and strongholds I needed to surrender. In the quiet, I felt the nudge to leave a ministry I had led for twenty years and step into an unsafe, unknown, uncertain new role. In the quiet, I was prompted to start a new ministry with a counter-intuitive strategy that could very easily fail.

But it does beg the question: What if you dare to turn off the distractions, unplug, and practice pursuing God in regular times of space and quiet? Might he meet you there? Get ready because in the stillness and the quiet, God will call you out. He will extend dangerous invitations to the kind of deep soul change that can lead to action. This doesn't happen in a fifteen-minute quiet time with a to-do list and an agenda.

So, here is a practical invitation:

- Once a month, take an entire day to unplug, shut off the external noise, quiet your mind, and listen.
- Schedule it. Get it on your calendar. Fight for it. All kinds of things will come up, and you will have to fight for this time. Be relentless. Be persistent. Make this a priority.
- Find your place. I'm a big believer in finding a place you are passionate about, a place you love going to, maybe a place where God has met you in the past. Where is that place for you? Remember it. Find it. Go there.

- Awaken your soul. Do something to get you going. Listen to music, hike or bike, write, or read a chapter from your favorite book. Do something that stirs you.
- Look back. Remember the moments that have been significant in the past, and then begin to cast your gaze forward.

I said this was a practical invitation but didn't say it was easy. We have a mantra at Harbor: Fight for SPACE. Carving out time for something as foreign as silence and space into our frustratingly loud world is a battle. Give yourself some grace in this. Seeking space is a different rhythm than you are used to. Developing this crucial habit will take practice and time, but half the battle is getting started. So begin. Put it on your calendar now. I'm serious. The rest of this book will do you no good unless you determine now to seek the quiet. Make this the beginning (or the renewal) of a journey that lasts a lifetime, a journey marked by the intentional pursuit of the still, small voice, the gentle whisper that is the one we most need to hear.

Be warned. I have no doubt that a dangerous vision, a dangerous hope, dangerous steps of faith, holy discontentment, and deep peace will be birthed in these extended times of quiet. If you can develop this rhythm of stillness and quiet, you will be dangerous to an enemy as well. If you practice the regular practice of taking time to be alone and quiet before God, you will have a much better chance of living with rhythm, leaving an intentional legacy, and staying the course in your faith, at work, and with your family. Then, you will be ready to step into whatever God has in store for you, however wild that may be.

*If you're new to taking extended times of SPACE and quiet, Harbor has resources you may find helpful. See the resource section at the end of this book.*

## Chapter 7: Stay Strong

> Ezra wept, prostrate in front of the Temple of God. As he prayed and confessed, a huge number of the men, women, and children of Israel gathered around him. All the people were now weeping as if their hearts would break. . . . 'We betrayed our God by marrying foreign wives from the people around here. But all is not lost; there is still hope for Israel. Let's make a covenant right now with our God . . . Now get up, Ezra. Take charge—we're behind you. Don't back down.'
>
> (Ezra 10:1-4, MSG)

True confession: I don't think I had ever read the book of Ezra in the Bible, so I missed the amazing stuff in these verses. Who knew that Tom Petty wasn't the first to write the phrase, "Don't back down"?

Israel is in trouble, facing fierce opposition from within and without. The people have again forgotten God and drifted into poor decisions and compromise. The superior power and dominating force of the day, Babylon, had beaten the Hebrews into total submission, leaving their land and the temple in utter ruins and banishing the people to exile. Now, more than a hundred years later, some of the Hebrew people are back in Jerusalem, trying to figure out what's next and what, if anything, they can do to reclaim their identity and find some hope in this dark time.

After many decades of silence and despair, Ezra enters the story. It's a story that has repeatedly played out for the Jewish people and is, in fact, playing out in our culture today. The people who pursue God are under attack from outside forces hell-bent on taking them out. But outside forces are not the only enemy at play then or now.

The people have forgotten God, likely in gradual, subtle ways. They have failed to make him the center of their lives. They have given way to compromise and various seductions from the culture. They've made deals and convinced themselves that their actions don't matter. Facing so much loss, I'm guessing they settled and decided to get whatever satisfaction they could. This slow fade from God in their personal lives came with serious consequences.

The landscape of Iceland is incredibly striking. It's hard to put into words with its expansive vistas and glacier-fed waterfalls. It is a collision of beauty and extremes—truly a land of fire and ice. And it has a mystic spiritual feel. Scattered throughout the vast, barren countryside, you see churches everywhere. There was a day when Christianity was the very heartbeat of the country. Missionaries planted churches, and fierce warrior monks from Ireland and northern England powerfully spread the gospel in this dark, cold land. I visited a lake fed by a hot spring where people were baptized hundreds of years ago. Choosing a hot spring was a great call by those doing the baptizing.

Can you imagine feeling called to bring God and the Christian faith to Iceland hundreds of years ago? Crossing the icy North Atlantic, building a house of stone in the mountainside for shelter, and then gathering a few people in this cold and often dark place? You can feel the sacrifice so many made in bringing a vibrant faith to Iceland. The striking thing about these churches scattered throughout the country is that they are no longer churches. They are largely community gathering spots and tourist attractions, nothing more. Iceland today, per capita, is one of the most unchurched countries in the world. The evidence of what happens when people fade away from God, sometimes in subtle ways that no one notices, is on full display in Iceland. For all of us, that fade from God can start with small decisions, seemingly insignificant moments of compromise, and movement away from God in individual journeys. Eventually, all those personal decisions multiply and impact things on a much bigger scale. Over time, an entire country has not only moved away from God but sees Christianity as irrelevant, certainly not something worth fighting for.

Sounds familiar, doesn't it?

Now we turn back to Ezra, who comes on the scene after decades of struggle in Israel. He is God's chosen man to bring truth and hope to a hurting people. As the story unfolds in Ezra 10, he and the people have returned to the site of the temple and are trying to restore some hope in a very dark moment in their history. We soon realize there is a route to hope and restoration, but it will not be easy. This passage lays out a pathway back toward God. Ezra engaged the people and restored humility, passion, and worship. He wept for and with the people and led them in confession and repentance. In verse one, we see Ezra fall prostrate before God, and the people follow his example, weeping as if their hearts would break. This is where the journey back begins. "Ezra wept, prostrate in front of The Temple of God. As he prayed and confessed, a huge number of the men, women, and children of Israel gathered around him. All the people were now weeping as if their hearts would break." (Ezra 10:1, MSG)

Then, there is action. They make a covenant, a promise to do this differently in the future. This is where it gets hard, really hard. The Hebrew people have gone against God's command to not marry outside their tribe. So now they must make the tough decision. Will they follow God even when it's unbearably hard? Even when it seems to make no sense? "But all is not lost; there is still hope for Israel. Let's make a covenant right now with our God, agreeing to get rid of all these wives and children, just as my master and those who honor God's commandment are saying. It's what The Revelation says, so let's do it." (Ezra 10:2-3, MSG) Wait a minute, let's get rid of these wives and children? That is no small task. That is a different level of hard. That is putting everything on the table so that they can stop this slow fade from God that has occurred over generations. And it begs a question for me: Am I ready to do what it takes to align my life with what God wants? What a challenge this story gives us.

So Israel makes some tough decisions to make things right. Ezra listened, confessed, and modeled a deep brokenness, and then acted on what he heard. But another key point in this story is that he was not alone. The people encouraged Ezra to get up, take charge, and lead. "Now get up, Ezra. Take charge—we're behind you. Don't back down." (Ezra 1:4, MSG) The people were more than present; they strengthened, challenged, and inspired Ezra, reminding him they would have his back. They urged him not to back down. He did not do this alone, and we cannot make the mistake of stepping out with no one in our corner.

Back in 2009, I faced an intense personal and leadership crisis. I was in San Diego with Ben and Kyle, the two young leaders who started Harbor Ministries with me. Given the intense, disheartening events happening in my family, I was ready to give up on the Harbor dream. It was an intensely difficult time, and I was completely drained, worn out, and disillusioned. I was angry and wondered if I could still follow a God who seemed to allow such evil to happen. I was sitting on the boardwalk on Mission Beach when a stranger approached and asked if I felt the peace of God at that moment. I ignored him. He was the last person on that beach I wanted to interact with, but he persisted. He put his hand on my shoulder and said he hoped that no matter what I faced, I could find God's peace. In that moment, things began to change. I will never forget that direct encounter with God on the Mission Beach boardwalk. It became a marker for my life going forward.

That morning Ben and Kyle leaned into the work I was too discouraged to do. They assured me they would help carry me through, they had my back, and they reminded me I was not in it alone. As I look back on that time, God did not spare me from the hurt, but he wildly sent a random stranger, a messenger with the exact words I needed to be assured that God was still with me. And through the words and presence of Ben and Kyle, he encouraged me to get back up, stay strong, and not back down.

We must remind ourselves often of Ezra 10:4. More than at any time in our history, we need men and women ready to stand up and face the intense opposition coming from so many directions. In this culture, we are well beyond a slow fade; we are in a rapid free-fall away from God. But it is not too late; there is hope, there is a pathway back, and we are not alone. And you are not alone as you read this. Now is the time to get up, take charge, hold our ground, and not back down.

## Chapter 8: Higher Ground

Moses is coming to the end of his leadership journey. For almost forty years, he has led the Hebrew people through this desert wilderness. Talk about a tough assignment! He led the entire nation out of Egypt, out of slavery, through the Red Sea, and right up to the Promised Land. Moses appoints twelve spies to scout out the land that God promised the Hebrews. Keep in mind these were the absolute best of the best, one strategic leader from each tribe. The twelve came back and reported that it was, in fact, a land as God promised: a place filled with rich resources and abundance. But there was a problem. Fierce enemies inhabited the Promised Land. Many of the leaders said that the people there were like giants and the Hebrews like grasshoppers.

Giants vs. grasshoppers.

Ten of the twelve spies gave way to fear. Only Joshua and Caleb stood in the gap, refused to back down, and believed they should take the land God had promised them. But the others caved, influenced the people, and caused belief and courage to crumble. The enemy that inhabited the land seemed too fierce and the obstacles too great, so the people gave into fear and again turned from God. And the consequences would cost them dearly. The result is forty years of wandering in the desert. God waits for the entire generation of people who backed down, who didn't stay the course, to die. That was Moses' assignment: lead the people through forty years in the desert wilderness until the entire generation dies. That is a tough calling.

Now Moses leads a new generation as they approach the Promised Land. As this story picks up, the Hebrews are locked in battle with the fierce Amalekites, who, in many ways, were some of the first terrorists. They followed the Hebrews and caused fear and anxiety by consistently killing the weak and others who fell behind the group. Now the Hebrews and Amalekites are in an all-out battle, and Moses senses that if they want to prevail, he and two trusted companions must join this fight themselves. So Moses, his brother Aaron, and Hur, the husband of Moses's older sister, seek higher ground.

It is an out-of-the-box strategy for sure—three older men climb a rugged cliff at Rephidim, about 750 feet above the valley floor, to get a full view of both armies. The text says that as long as Moses has his arms raised, the Hebrew people advance, but when his arms are lowered, the Hebrews fall back in defeat. What a wild story!

Why was seeking higher ground critical? The people needed to see Moses, and I think the enemy needed to see him as well. The sight of Moses raising that staff and the Hebrews advancing had to strike fear in the heart of the Amalekites. The Hebrews needed the encouragement and inspiration seeing their leader brought. And what about Moses? Higher ground provided perspective. He could see the entire battle from that vantage point and get clarity about what needed to happen and what was at stake.

But what else was going on here with this story? Is it really about Moses raising his arms, or does it represent something more? Does it indicate that, yes, there is a battle raging in the valley below, but there is a more intense spiritual battle to be won or lost? In fact, it is in the fierce spiritual battle where things will be truly won or lost. Once again, Moses stands in the gap, absorbs the hits, and powerfully takes on the enemy on behalf of the people. Only when Moses sought higher ground did this come into focus.

And what about that staff Moses holds? This is the same staff Moses had in his hands years earlier at the burning bush. It's the same staff that Moses took to Pharaoh and used to work miracles. The staff Moses held to part the Red Sea is the same staff he held high above the battlefield to remind the people that they cannot doubt God or turn back to fear. The staff is a constant reminder that God, not Moses, is at work here.

Visualize for a moment what it looks like from the valley below. Moses stands on high ground, two trusted old friends, each holding up one of his arms to make the shepherd's rod visible. Moses on higher ground changes the battle. It changes everything.

I have found that seeking higher ground, stepping out, and moving toward the edge brings huge benefits. Higher ground has provided me with life, adventure, and much-needed perspective. I have found higher ground on the trail above Crested Butte, Colorado; venturing the edge of the Reykjanes lighthouse in Iceland; atop a small bluff overlooking the Platte River in eastern Nebraska; biking the top of a plateau overlooking Golden, Colorado. Sometimes, just seeing the horizon and the view from my front porch at sunset has provided inspiration and perspective. I do believe seeking a literal higher ground is critical. From higher ground, I can:

- Get needed perspective.
- Find renewed passion and encouragement.
- Gain strength and courage.

- More easily see the next steps and pathways forward that I just can't see in the valley.
- Gain new ideas, new energy, and needed inspiration.
- Be in a place of peace where I am reminded that God has got this.

It is so much easier to stay low. Sometimes higher ground is dangerous, it can be a struggle to get there, and it almost always involves some element of pain to make it. But if we can press on through the pain and discomfort, the journey can be filled with anticipation, joy, and even hope. The thing is when we find that higher ground, we have to be willing to pause, wait and stay there. Edges and risk are almost always involved. As we shift our conversation from stay to wild, keep in mind that when you feel lost, or confused, seek some higher ground. It can be the best place to get the inspiration you need and can give the best view to see where you've come from and where you're going.

# Part 2:
# Wild

## Chapter 9: Disruption

They call Iceland the land of fire and ice. The landscape is shaped by retreating glaciers and active volcanoes. There are thirty-two active volcanic systems in a country roughly the geographic size of Kentucky. According to VisitIceland.com, A volcano erupts in Iceland once every four years on average. When Eyjafjallajökull erupted in April 2010, the smoke and ash virtually shut down air travel in Europe. In 2022, satellite cameras captured haunting images of an underwater eruption. Iceland is a place where the land melts and the earth trembles.

It is unbelievably beautiful. And wild.

It is alluring, captivating, disruptive, unsettling.

And I'm drawn to it.

A particular cliff in Iceland has become symbolic of Harbor and the faith steps we challenge leaders to take. Every few years, we invite alumns of our leadership journeys to travel to Iceland and to this cliff. One trip was scheduled for 2020. First, COVID restrictions delayed us twice. Then our plans were disrupted again by a volcanic eruption. This trip and Iceland itself are microcosms of how the world feels today: disrupted. Fully disrupted.

We feel the tremors in nearly all aspects of life. Life has changed, and now we must figure out how to live in a badly shaken world, in a country and world we often don't recognize and that so often make no sense. People have that look in their eyes, the look you see on the Weather Channel after a tornado or flood rips through a town. They seem to be asking where they will find stability. Where do we look for the strength and courage to live in uncertainty? I cling to these words:

> "My help and glory are in God—granite-strength and safe-Harbor God." (Psalm 62:7, MSG)

In more than three decades of ministry, I have never seen such anxiety and stress grip people as I do today. We've been traumatized by the shifting dynamics in culture, politics, and health and all the conflict and hate in this country and the world. But here's the thing: Disruption can be important, it can lead to depth, the right kind of dependence, and it can be a catalyst for needed change.

Years before the pandemic and global upheaval we're experiencing today, we chose the word disrupt as the focus for the season of work we were doing at Harbor Ministries. We talked about disruption. We embraced it. We told the Harbor story in a booklet that opened with the line, "God is all about disruption. Think about that for a second."

Beyond nature, we can look at God's word and see that disruption is a constant. The Bible is filled with accounts of people whose lives were changed, altered, disrupted after encounters with God. After forty days alone in the desert, strengthening and readying himself for a three-year run that would change the world, Jesus emerges and begins to build his team. As he walks the shores of the Sea of Galilee, he sees two brothers. Peter and Andrew, working the family fishing business. This is how they survive, how they eat, how they support their families. Fishing is their whole life. Then Jesus says, "Come, follow me," and everything changes. Jesus continues down the shore and sees two other brothers in a boat with their father mending nets. James and John leave their nets, their boat, and their father behind and go with Jesus. Disruption. Upheaval. They had no idea of the wild adventure ahead.

Jesus interrupts the status quo of his day. He walks into the temple just a week before his death and sees religious leaders who have sold out to profit. Jesus doesn't just disrupt; he causes a panic, a riot even. He cracks a whip, turns over tables, and clears the temple in what has to be described as an aggressive, passionate display of defending truth. This isn't the Jesus I learned about when I was young. The picture I stared at every Sunday was a calm, docile Jesus sitting on a hill taking in the view. But this Jesus in the temple was a passionate, all-in leader who was not going to compromise, settle in, and let things pass. He disrupted life as usual in a big way.

And how about Paul? He is largely responsible for the stoning death of Steven, and he has been commissioned by the leaders of the day to destroy this new movement of Christ followers. He travels back to Jerusalem to continue his campaign, but God knocks him off his mule, blinds him with bright light, and speaks directly to him. For three days, Paul is blind and does not eat. It seems he needs to see things differently so he and the world can be changed.

In the Old Testament, we find disruption in the stories of Esther, Jonah, and Jonathan, to name just a few. Esther is blessed with beauty and a presence so captivating and compelling that the Persian king makes this common Hebrew his queen. When a counselor to the king begins to lay out his plan to destroy the Hebrews, Esther has a choice. She can say nothing and continue to live in comfort and safety. It would be easy to convince herself there will be other moments when she will be needed, so why risk her status now? Or she can risk her status, her lifestyle, wealth, privilege, and even her life to stand up for her people. Esther takes a step and enters the king's court, a move which can mean certain death for any woman if the king does not receive her. She pleads with the king on behalf of the Hebrews. The king listens, and instead of Hebrews dying, the counselor is killed. God gave Esther a gift and then fully disrupted her life so she could stand in the gap for something much bigger than herself.

The last place in the world Jonah wants to go is Nineveh. So he tries everything he can to avoid what God has told him to do. It is way more comfortable where he is at. It's predictable. Safe. But soon, in his avoidance of God, Jonah is swallowed by a whale and spit out on the shore. It took that kind of disruption to get his attention, to cause Jonah to change course and accept a dangerous assignment to a dangerous place.

Jonathan is the eldest son of King Saul. Since becoming king, Saul has slowly followed his own path instead of God's. Pride, power, and control have eroded his leadership. They say ultimate power ultimately corrupts, which was certainly the case with Saul. God's hand was no longer with him. Now, a massive enemy force has gathered. We find Saul's army hiding behind rocks and hunkering down in caves, afraid to engage the enemy.

The Philistine army had 5,000 chariots, 2,000 horsemen, and "foot soldiers as numerous as sand on the seashore." (1 Samuel 13:5) In modern terms, that would be like having 5,000 armored vehicles, 2,000 fighter jets, and a force of foot soldiers too numerous to count. No wonder Saul's army is hiding in fear.

But Jonathan has had enough. He is tired of seeing his dad sit on his ass and do nothing while his army hides. Jonathon knows what God can do. He remembers the things God has done in the past. He knows that nothing is impossible if God goes before them. So Jonathan asks his young armor-bearer to accompany him to the garrison and engage the enemy in battle. In 1 Samuel 14:6, Jonathan says this famous line: "Perhaps God will be with us." Jonathan understands that safety is not guaranteed, but he needs to do something. Perhaps God will be with us. Jonathan clearly steps into this moment without his ducks in a row and with no promised outcome. He just knows God can do this, and he must act. So, he and his armor-bearer take on the enemy's strongest position, call them out, subdue them, and gain higher ground. At one point, Jonathan and his young arms bearer are on all fours, scrambling up this hill to engage a far superior enemy. They win the day, and their actions inspire the army, which rallies to defeat the Philistines. Jonathan disrupted the course of the battle. Just two men stepped out, chose action instead of safety, and changed the course of history.

It does seem that God uses disruption, whether he causes it or whether he uses it, to bring the change and purposes he desires. Many times in my life, change happened after the ground shook under me. And almost always the result has been a deeper impact and a closer, more authentic walk with him.

We need a roadmap to help us stay wild in a fully disrupted world. So often, everything in us wants us to pull back, settle in, and play it safe. And this urge only increases as we age and the layers and complexities of life keep coming at us. But that may be the most dangerous thing we can do. It is a soul-killing way to live, and I don't believe that's what God had in mind.

> I'll walk through fire
>
> Step into the unknown
>
> Jump in the deep end
>
> I'm born to stay wild
>
> I've faced the heartache
>
> I've walked a lonely road
>
> Towards something greater
>
> I'm born to stay wild

-Bryan Oelsen, "Stay Wild"

We need to be men and women with staying power ***and*** wildness in our lives and faith journeys so we can impact a shaken world desperate to find hope. In the first portion of this book, we talked about how to stay rooted in God despite our circumstances. Now, we'll explore how to stay wild. Relevant. Alive. Engaged in God's call to something bigger than ourselves. I hope we will learn to embrace wonder, explore, chase a few cliffs, and even have fun along the way.

Are you ready?

## Chapter 10: Lean In

Over these last few years, so much of our instinct and natural reaction says to step back and try to insulate ourselves from some of the hard.

*Life is chaotic enough as it is. Why make it worse?*

*Maybe if I stay in my lane and don't make too many waves, things will get better or at least not deteriorate further.*

*I know how to navigate where I am, but I don't have the capacity if things get more complicated.*

*I'll hunker down, avoid risk whenever possible, and stay safe.*

Many years ago, we had a family reunion in Colorado. At the time, our oldest son was just three. The entire family decided to go on an afternoon rafting trip. The guides assured me it was a calm river and that our three-year-old would be fine. The guide told us he had rafted all over the world and had never once been thrown from the raft. Somehow, we believed the guide, and you know how it goes. It was our firstborn, and I was excited to have him experience everything with us. We did not want him to miss out. The problem was these class-one rapids had changed overnight, and everyone seemed unaware. Our guide gave us instructions, telling us the most critical thing to remember is that if we head toward a boulder or rock in the river, we must lean in. "All your instincts will be to lean away from the rock, but that's the worst thing you can do."

So we left shore, and within a couple of minutes, we realized it was a mistake. The problem was that they had released extra water from the Taylor Park Reservoir that day, and the river was running faster by the minute. Drew's fear and tears increased with every

bump, and soon we were heading for a large boulder in the mi… of the river. Most of us in the raft were concerned for Drew and leaned toward him as we hit. The raft wrapped around the rock and then released. It was like a slingshot that catapulted the guide into the river. The rest of us made it through, but it cost the guide his reputation and made him the focus of many jokes from his peers the rest of the day.

Leaning into the rock was critical, and we missed it. It is human nature to step back from problems, lean away, avoid them, or try to manage them. But leaning into whatever obstacle we find in our path can keep us safer and steadier, even in the most turbulent times. In March 2020, the world was filled with so much fear and uncertainty I wondered if Harbor Ministries would survive. Like everything else, all our programming was shutting down, and we were not sure the funds would still come in. But one thing we found ourselves thinking about was how we could keep our tribe encouraged. How could we still invest in them when everything we had set in motion was now in jeopardy? What came out of the time were some creative initiatives we would have never undertaken apart from the pandemic: music, writing, and a podcast. The podcast we hoped would encourage hundreds has now reached tens of thousands. This podcast, SPACE by Harbor Ministries, has become a tool to help many stay steady and grounded while maintaining a wild pursuit of God and all he has for them. We invested in music and an album called *Safe Harbor* and developed numerous written resources to help people find God in space, solitude, and quiet. I am not sure any of this radical investment in people would have happened if we had not leaned into the disruptive events of the last few years.

…r continued to advance during that dark …e honest: there was a cost. Many times in …s, I struggled with fear and uncertainty. So many …ke pulling back, hiding, and certainly not taking any r… time and again, God nudged me to step out, lean in, and keep moving forward.

I recently read the book *The Comfort Crisis*, which referenced studies that provide strong evidence that people are at their very best when they encounter significant discomfort. Scientists are finding that types of discomfort can actually protect us from certain diseases and help keep stress, anxieties, and even death at bay.[4]

That's intriguing and totally makes sense to me. In perhaps the most comfortable country in the world, we face high suicide rates, heartbreaking gun violence, skyrocketing rates of depression and anxiety, and so much anger. Might it be true that pushing ourselves out of our physical, emotional, and spiritual comfort zones could sharpen and strengthen us? Maybe it is not so complicated. Pushing ourselves outside the box, outside of what we are used to, forces us to innovate, create, make new memories, and adapt. Those moments of discomfort can keep us mentally sharp, physically stretched, and spiritually attuned.

In that summer of 2020 (the first COVID summer), I invested in a new mountain bike. It was a hot, dry season in Nebraska. I became addicted to my new bike, and it helped me cope with the decisions and uncertainty that were pressing in on me. My favorite time to hit the trail was in the heat of the day. For some reason pushing myself in the heat became fuel, and the more I did it, the more it strengthened me. Some studies suggest that working out in the heat has physical benefits that extend beyond the exercise. I wish I could say I kept that intensity up or that I continued to lean into discomfort, but over time, it was so easy to settle in and fall back into old routines that did not push me out of my comfort zones.

So are there some old routines you need to break?

What are some ways you can nudge or push yourself out of your comfort zone?

Is there something you are passionate about that you haven't made time for? Could you put your time and resources there?

Is there anything you can change physically or spiritually that could help sharpen and strengthen you?

What is God asking you to lean into?

What's holding you back?

## Chapter 11: Terrifically Alive

Even though Harbor teaches and practices living with rhythm, there are times when my reserves get low. I was preparing to travel between Harbor events in California and Colorado. I would need energy and passion to pour into leaders who had gathered from all over the country. How could I be ready for the busy stretch in front of me? My heart and spirit needed things that give me life: slow mornings with extended time in nature and music. So every day for two weeks, I cleared my calendar of early morning appointments, and I was either on my bike or in my kayak, slowing down and renewing my soul. Some mornings, I did not feel like making the effort to load the kayak or bike, but I made myself do it. And with each day that passed, I could sense the impact of being in nature and connecting with those things that have brought me such life over the years.

Those two weeks ended with the impromptu trip to Colorado for the Marcus Mumford concert I described earlier. As I watched Marcus perform away from the big crowds, alone with an acoustic guitar, I wondered if he, too, was trying to reconnect with his why and his passion. He had filled stadiums all over the world with Mumford and Sons. Yet here he was in a small theatre in front of a few hundred people, playing his acoustic. The words "you were born to meet your maker" never seemed more real.

Those few days of intentionally slowing and then doing something unscheduled that didn't make a whole lot of sense restored my passion for the mission of encouraging and inspiring strategic leaders. I remembered why we started Harbor Ministries believing we could change the world by radically investing in just a few leaders at a time. I recalled the stories and the recent impact of the groups we were working with. I remembered how God was in all of it and I felt alive and ready!

God's promise for us is LIFE! Not a comfortable life or even a safe life, but a full, rich, abundant life. To experience that, I believe we must stay deeply connected to those people, places, and experiences that are life-giving.

I'm reminded of Ezekiel 47. In the middle of the passage, verse nine reads, "Where the river flows, life will flourish." Another translation says, "Where the river flows, everything will live." This is a beautiful picture of what God wants for us. The Bible references rivers many times as life-giving, inspiring places. God wants us to live from that place. Even in hard times, even when difficulties are all around us, he still wants us to live through those life-giving moments.

There is a house in Estes Park we call the Blue Spruce Manor. We refer to it as the anchor site for Harbor Ministries. The Big Thompson River runs right behind the house, so close you could fish from the deck. There is something about being that close to that water. It's relaxing, refreshing, inspiring. I find it easy to breathe deeply and soak in the moments. The constant movement of the water brings clarity, perspective, and focus. And it is a great visual of what God wants for us in our relationship with him.

I hope God will take you to that kind of place in your own story. Where is a place that brings that kind of refreshment and is life-giving for you?

I'm a big fan of Tom Petty's music, and many of his songs have found their way into the Harbor leadership journeys. So in the summer of 2022, we took a chance and invited Steve Ferrone, the drummer of the Heartbreakers, to join my right-hand guy, Bryan Olesen, and his band at a fundraiser. It was a night to have fun, celebrate, and honor Petty's music. The evening was a risk (Why would a guy who had played Wembley and the Super Bowl come to Lincoln, Nebraska?) and part of our commitment to staying wild. It filled my soul. I think the event might have been life-giving for Steve Ferrone as well. At least I hope so.

One of the night's many highlights was right before the band came on stage. At any concert, there is a buzz as the crowd anticipates the opening song. That was true even in our small venue with several hundred people. The energy was palpable, and my adrenaline was sky-high.

What brings you that kind of energy, that kind of life?

What fuels your passion?

When you find those things, run toward them. Invest in them. That Tom Petty tribute night gave me fuel for a long time. We need those life-giving moments so we can be at our best for the rest of what life throws at us. I hope as you read this, something stirs within you. I hope you'll be reminded of something life-giving from your past or something you have been dreaming about or hoping for.

Let's take a longer look at Ezekiel 47 about a place of life.

> He told me, 'This water flows east, descends to the Arabah and then into the sea, the sea of stagnant waters. When it empties into those waters, the sea will become fresh. Wherever the river flows, life will flourish.'
>
> (Ezekiel 47:8, MSG)

The following verse describes fishermen standing side-by-side, shoulder-to-shoulder, along the shore, casting their nets as the water teems with all kinds of fish. It's an image of joy and abundance. Of life!

Even with the hardships present in a fully disrupted world, we need life! It's okay, even necessary, to enjoy the moments, to have fun, to celebrate. When I'm able to find those places that bring life, energy, and passion, it brings out the kid in me. I am a better person, better to those around me, and more focused on my work. And when struggles do come, I have a better reserve, and things don't as easily throw me off course.

In 2 Corinthians 6, Paul is trying to encourage the people not to give up and not hold back, no matter what obstacles and opposition come their way. He wants them to stay the course. Now Paul knew something about intense, relentless opposition, and it's evident in this passage.

> People are watching us as we stay at our post, alertly, unswervingly . . . in hard times, tough times, bad times; when we're beaten up, jailed, and mobbed; working hard, working late, working without eating, with pure heart, clear head, steady hand; in gentleness, holiness, and honest love . . . when we're praised and when we're blamed; slandered, and honored; true to our word, though distrusted; ignored by the world but recognized by God; *terrifically alive*, though rumored to be dead; beaten within an inch of our lives, but refusing to die; immersed in tears, yet always filled with deep joy.
>
> (2 Corinthians 6:3-10, MSG, Emphasis ours)

So beaten, doubted, working relentlessly, rumored to be dead but *terrifically alive*! Man, this passage is such a picture of life, isn't it? If we are going to stay wild as we navigate all of this, we need to fight for ways to have that deep joy. We must find those things that help us stay terrifically alive through it all.

What is that for you? What are some of the things that bring both deep and surface-level joy?

What are the things that make you laugh and are just plain fun?

What might stir your soul and make you terrifically alive, even in the middle of oppressive circumstances?

One of the things I've been reminded of these last few weeks is my passion for taking people on a creative journey that has markers and moments that will create movement and deep change in their lives. I love inviting people into something different, something mysterious and adventurous, something that reflects the character of God.

This love for inviting others into experiences emerged when I was young. I was always the one who organized events and wanted to mark the moments, even on our family vacations. I was a notorious scrapbooker—I prefer to call them "travel journals now. As a little guy, I would take the pictures, capture the moments, and save them in my travel journal. I still love doing that today. I can't wait to invite people back to a ROGUE or RHYTHM event, though I've done more than ninety events with hundreds of leaders from around the country. It still helps me feel terrifically alive.

And, if you haven't guessed, music brings me life. Unfortunately, this passion took a hit in 2020 and 2021, but I've resolved that when I can take the time and spend the needed resources, I will find the concerts and seek out the music that gives me joy.

In our disrupted world, we're all dealing with uncertainty, struggle, and pain. So many of us carry layers of stress, worry, and fear. In the 1985 movie, *The Breakfast Club*, a group of teens spend a Saturday in detention. They begin to bond and are talking about their parents when one of the characters describes their dad as someone who just goes through the motions, has settled, and lost his passion. "When you grow up, your heart dies," the character Allison says.

We can't let that happen. The world needs us to live from a different place. We need to find things that awaken us.

So what is it for you? Pause now and consider what awakens you.

What stirs your heart?

What makes you come to life, even when you're facing really hard things?

No excuses here. We are called to be people who are terrifically alive. Life is too short to settle, simply to keep our heads down and keep grinding; it's too short to lose our hearts along the way.

So, if you journal, this is the time to get that journal and remind yourself of some of the stories of your past, some of the moments that gave you life. Capture some of the times you felt like a kid again. Then decide how you will do what it takes to enter that space.

My friend Bryan Olesen, who has been with me in Harbor Ministries over this last decade, wrote a song, "One Shot One Life."

> I'm getting closer to the edge
>
> No turning back no giving in

Running away from who I've been

With every step against the wind. I just wanna feel alive.

. . . I won't let this fear keep me from living

I just wanna feel alive

. . . I've only got one shot

One shot, one life.

-Bryan Olesen, "One Shot One Life"

And don't forget fun! In Harbor Ministries we challenge leaders to find a good rhythm that includes work and action, space, and play. I believe that the men and women who are difference-makers in life have figured out how to infuse a healthy dose of all those in their day-to-day and month-to-month routines. So many men I work with have no problem investing themselves deeply in their work. They find purpose and acceptance from themselves and others there. When we feel like we are failing at other things, maybe struggling in relationships, it's easy to throw ourselves into work. And work is important for sure, but not at the price of sacrificing fun—good old-fashioned fun. I remember one of our events with a group of high-level executive leaders. We had a spirited discussion on this idea of play and fun. Some in the group felt F-U-N was a weak word that somehow needed to be strengthened. Perhaps we need a better word for this idea of investing in things that bring laughter and joy—things that keep us terrifically alive.

Do you remember when you were young? What were some of the things that you lost yourself in? What could you spend hours doing? What caused you to lose track of time and be absorbed in the activity? Music, hours of basketball with friends, fishing, and exploring are all fun for me.

Don't dismiss this idea. Think about the last time you laughed a deep, resonant belly laugh. When do you let your guard down, shut off the phone, and do something just because you enjoy it? Why not try it now?

## Chapter 12: Embrace Wonder

If we are going to stay wild in our pursuit of God and all this life has to offer, it will help to open our eyes to the wonder around us. My online dictionary tells me that wonder is "a feeling of surprise mingled with admiration, caused by something beautiful, unexpected, unfamiliar, or inexplicable."

I took my first trip to Iceland several years ago with my two sons and some of the guys who helped launch Harbor. We went to find that cliff. It is a land filled with wonder. On my last trip there, I went a few days early. We decided to make the six-mile hike to the volcano that had erupted just a few weeks earlier. This was a big challenge for me physically. The first few miles had a steep grade, and the rest of the group was well ahead of me. More than once, I thought about quitting. The piercing question was whether I would keep putting one foot in front of the other. With no one to encourage me, did I have the grit to keep going?

Then I looked across the steamy lava field that filled the landscape as far as I could see. I felt like I was living out a scene from *Lord of the Rings: Return of the King*. It looked and felt like a portion of Frodo and Sam's journey toward Mordor. This thought helped convince me I was on an epic journey and needed to press on. I knew I would likely never get a chance like this again.

The steep grade eventually leveled off to a difficult mile through black lava rock, where I had to watch every step. The steamy lava field continued down the valley, but the smoke and anticipation were building. Gray clouds and light rain persisted as I reached a slick, muddy decline. I will never forget rounding the last corner and seeing the active lava flow so close to the volcano's main vent.

There is no way words can describe it. It was violent, unnerving, awe-inspiring, mesmerizing, unpredictable, and beautiful all at the same time.

We sat in silence and awe for a very long time. I could have stayed there all day. Under the surface, I could sense the movement and hear the roar. We were so close we could feel the heat from the lava flow. It was like being on a cliff and hearing a roaring, rugged ocean beneath us, only more powerful and much deeper. There was a depth to this roar and an unsettling yet intoxicating movement that felt like it was coming from the center of the earth. I'd never experienced anything like it.

And I was so close to not experiencing it. It would have been much easier and, in some ways, made more sense for me to pass on that hike and spend the time preparing for the group on its way to meet us in Iceland. But taking the step, pursuing wild things, pushing myself, and embracing moments as they came readied me not only for that trip but for whatever was ahead. The only way to experience this volcano in this incredible way was to work my way up that steep grade, follow that difficult and rocky summit, follow the trail of steam and lava. I had to make that hike. That volcano breathed life back into me in ways I cannot fully describe. I was both exhausted and exhilarated. I sat for hours in total wonder.

There are times like this hike when you need to press on, take that difficult next step, and keep moving. In the midst of that movement, God can surprise us with indescribable moments of wonder. At other times, we simply need to stay alert and pause when a moment is upon us. Several years ago my wife and I were on a weekend getaway in Colorado. As we came out of our cabin to

head to dinner, we stopped in our tracks. We felt the warmth from the sun setting under a line of clouds. Even though it was warm and clear overhead, snow was blowing in from distant clouds. The aspens were bright yellow, and the colors on the distant mountain as we looked toward the sunset were spectacular. It was like the sky was opening up and giving us a glimpse into something deeper—this great collision of warm and cold, snow and sunshine, gray and vibrant colors. This amazing moment was offered to us just because we paused and lingered.

It certainly does not need to be as dramatic as a hike to a volcano. In many ways this idea of wonder is a state of mind, a sense of gratefulness and anticipation, and a commitment to fully living in the moment. Webster's definition of wonder rings true: "a feeling of surprise, mingled with admiration, caused by something unexpected, unfamiliar or inexplicable." That sounds like worship to me. So in the days ahead consider wonder. Be content to be still.

Pause and linger at the next sunset.

Get yourself in front of some great art.

Turn off the exterior noise and listen to your favorite song.

Read something that has stirred you in the past.

Stare at the stars a little longer.

Sit by that creek.

Don't cast your line so quickly that you forget to enjoy the catch.

Take extra time on your next hike or bike ride. Don't forget to celebrate the moments as they come.

Please don't lose your sense of wonder. Stay curious. Ask God to give you the eyes of a child with the ability to lay down some of your worries and stress as you explore this world. And remember to focus not just on the creation but the creator.

## Chapter 13: Wide-open Spaces

You don't have to travel all the way to Iceland to embrace wonder. I have often found wildness and renewed life in the wide-open spaces closer to home.

Recently I had a tough week filled with difficult conversations. So many people around me were going through tough things. Then there were discussions with people who have very strong opinions on things I disagree with. It was all taking a toll, and I was discouraged. I lost my perspective. I got caught up in small stories. It took me back to a time several years ago when I was stuck in deep disappointment and struggle. And at the time, my youngest son was going through significant physical battles that cost him some of his biggest dreams. My wife finally told me I needed to get away and regain some perspective. At the same time, one of our Harbor alums sent me a random message that included this line:

> *There are times in life you need to enter the wide-open spaces, if nothing else, to breathe in new air in search of a new way forward.*

Message received. I decided to take it literally and hit the wide-open spaces of southern Wyoming and northern Colorado. Honestly, I was less in search of wonder and more ready to have it out with God.

I took my bike and headed up to a trail near Steamboat, Colorado, where I had ridden many times. But this time felt different. I was riding with such anger and frustration. As I approached an upper meadow, I rode to a large rock and collapsed. I had it out with God on the rock. I yelled out my frustrations and anger. And I stayed there. I sat with all those feelings in the middle of the wonder of God's creation. The longer I sat, the more I sensed that

I couldn't leave that rock until I let it all go. I was there for hours partly because I didn't want to give up control. That moment exposed my fear of trusting God. I couldn't understand how God had let such hard things happen to my family. So I stayed.

Eventually, as I looked out over the valley toward Steamboat Springs, I had a moment of simple clarity: I'm either going to trust God, even in this dark time, or I'm not. And a whole lot rested on where I would land with that simple question. The next moment is hard to describe. I let it go. I released control. I swear I felt fifty pounds lighter on the next stretch of the ride.

That moment would never have happened had I not entered the wide-open spaces and wrestled with God on his turf.

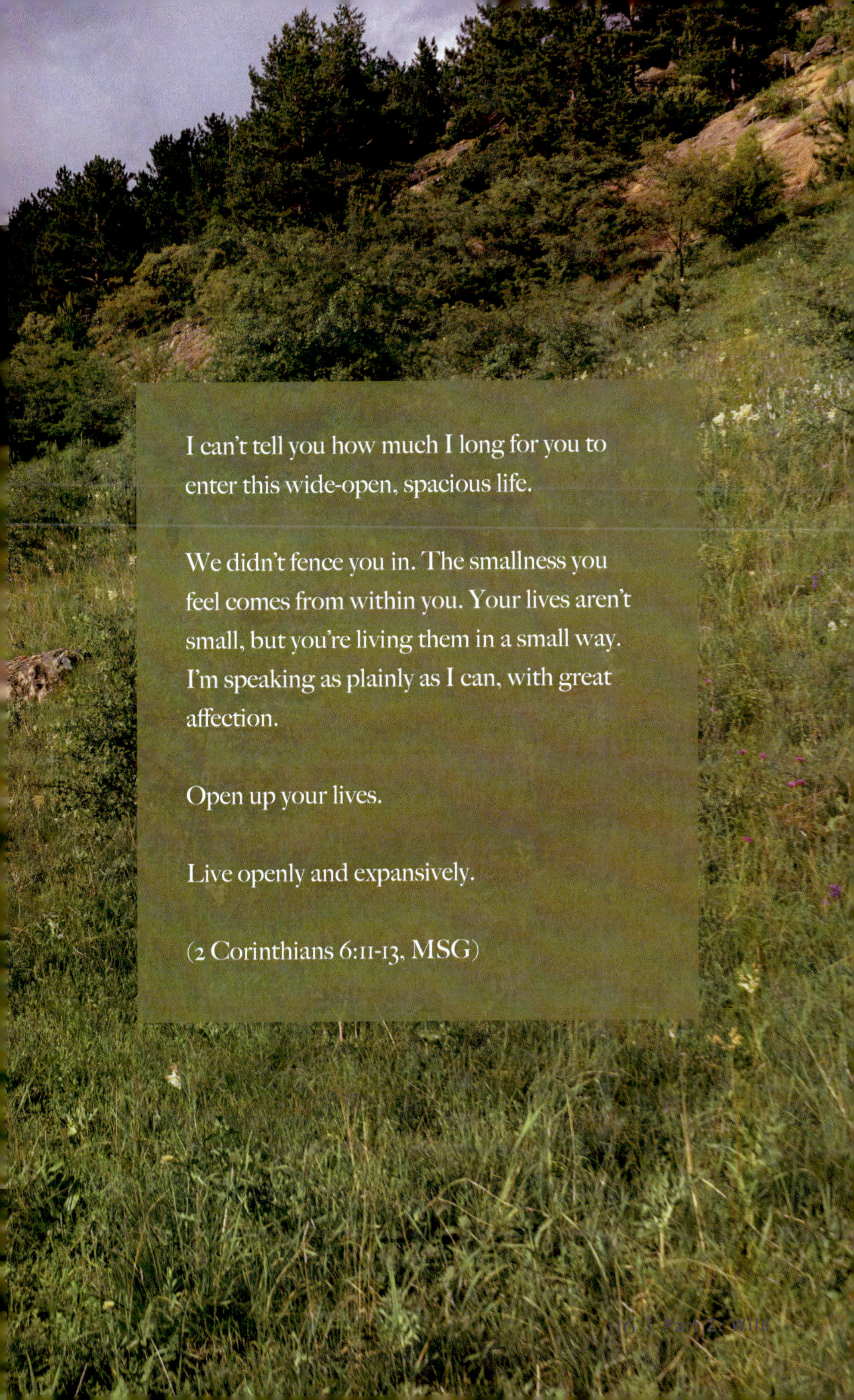

I can't tell you how much I long for you to enter this wide-open, spacious life.

We didn't fence you in. The smallness you feel comes from within you. Your lives aren't small, but you're living them in a small way. I'm speaking as plainly as I can, with great affection.

Open up your lives.

Live openly and expansively.

(2 Corinthians 6:11-13, MSG)

Don't rush off the rock. Sit here with these words. Read the passage two or three times.

What is God saying? What is he inviting you into?

Don't just think of wide-open spaces in a physical way. Have you been stuck in a way of thinking, maybe a view of God, that needs to be opened up?

Consider people with different views, theologies, and thoughts and see if there are some new ways for you to think about things.

Take a look at people from different cultures and countries and marvel at some of the attributes of the one who created them.

I am convinced we have an enemy who wants us to live in small stories. Too often, we have a narrow view of God. We have put him into a box. But is it possible this wild, mysterious creator cannot be tamed, contained, or controlled? Is there a practical step you can take, like reading something that will push and challenge you to think about things differently?

Could you get yourself to a place that reminds you that you are part of a much bigger story?

Wide-open spaces might be close to home, or you might need to take a little road trip to a place that brings perspective or helps you get unstuck. I find when I get to these places, I gain clarity. It's easier to see my way through the dark times and even begin to dream again.

Take the words of 2 Corinthians 6 with you to the wide-open spaces and see what God does.

## Chapter 14: Stay Passionate

I mentioned earlier that I recently went to the movie *Jesus Revolution*. I feel like I need to make a disclaimer. I generally avoid Christian movies because so many have been cheesy and, to me, miss the heart of people and often God's core message. But *Jesus Revolution* was different, at least for me. I am still unsure why, but I was deeply emotional for days after seeing it. It awakened something in me. Maybe it was the simple power of a great story. So often we can neglect the power in our own story. This may be a good time to set this book down and think over the previous year or even the last few months.

How has God shown up in your story?

What were some thin place moments when God's story intersected with your own?

As you reflect, are there any themes that emerge?

Maybe *Jesus Revolution* impacted me because many in my family became spiritually alive in the early seventies through the Jesus movement documented in the film. My mom was a bit of a mystic. She believed God could speak to us through dreams, movies, nature, and just the everyday moments of life. She could sense his leading and promptings, and she would act on them. One story she told was about sensing God tell her to drop what she was doing and drive thirty minutes to see a woman who was making a wedding dress for my sister. When Mom arrived, she found the woman pale, distraught, and prepared to end her own life that morning. My mom's willingness to pause, listen, step out of her own agenda, respond, and engage in someone's story changed everything that morning.

A few months ago, I found a letter in an old file that one of my best friends had written forty years ago after hearing my mom speak. Kathy wrote, "Sunday I heard one of the best speakers I have ever heard. She talked about twelve different ways God speaks to us and she had amazing personal examples of each one. Her bottom line was that God will speak to us individually just as we need it, if we can just stay connected to him."

My mom did not have a big audience; she was a housewife who lived in the country, but a woman who was determined to wildly pursue God and make the most of her days. She has been gone almost thirty years now, but as I reflect, I see so much of how I experience God and lead others today came from her. And her spiritual awakening came from this moment in the early seventies. She really did seem to hear God's voice so clearly. In many ways, she led my dad and many others into their own spiritual awakenings. My sister and now brother-in-law were both deeply impacted by this wild Jesus movement of the early 1970s as well.

So this particular movie may have had an impact on me because of that history. It could also be the parallels between the sixties and early seventies and our culture today. Or was it the stories and raw side of leadership that the movie highlighted so well? Time and time again throughout history, God has used gifted yet deeply flawed men and women to impact the world. And as this movie illustrated, he used broken people to launch one of our nation's most significant spiritual revivals.

Maybe it was the moments of awakening that changed lives, the compelling strength and voices of the men and women God used, or the simple truth that everyone, no matter what you have done or are doing, and no matter what has been done to you, is important and significant. So as I consider this idea of staying passionate, one line near the end of the movie resonates.

The central character, a pastor, has made some mistakes. He has a fractured relationship with the hippie character God used to change his life and who, in many ways, was the heart of this Jesus movement. The pastor is struggling and wonders if he has the passion and ability to continue because he has messed things up in so many ways. At that critical moment, his wife says, "Don't be so arrogant to think God can't work through your failures."

Staying passionate in my pursuit of God and his calling for my life has often been feast or famine. At times, I am ready to advance, no matter the obstacles. I'm ready to invest deeply in people and take the next mountain. There are those seasons when I feel so close to God and realize my relationship with him is what he really cares about. It's far more important than what I can do for him.

But often, there are desert times when my passion has dried up, times I am ready to fall back or simply settle in and coast. My heart is dulled, and I wonder if God is even there. It seems so hard to find him. Why are those thin place moments—the ones I'm so passionate about that I wrote a book on them—why are those places where heaven and earth collide so rare?

Why can I not have more consistency and a better rhythm to all of it?

In 2 Kings 13, we find a story about King Joash and the last days of the prophet Elisha. Elisha has blessed this king and his leadership time and time again. As another round of enemies closes in, Joash knows he needs the prophet's blessing. It seems the king's heart has drifted from God, and any blessing he can get through this old prophet is his best and only shot at staying relevant as a leader.

So as Joash approaches Elisha, this old prophet gives this king a fascinating test:

> . . . Joash the king of Israel came down to him, and wept over him and said, 'My father, my father, the chariots of Israel and its horsemen!' And Elisha said to him, 'Take a bow and arrows.' So he took a bow and arrows. Then *Elisha* said to the king of Israel, 'Lay your hand on the bow.' And he laid his hand *on it*, then Elisha put his hands on the king's hands. And he said, 'Open the window toward the east,' and he opened *it*. Then Elisha said, 'Shoot!' So he shot. And he said, 'The Lord's arrow of victory, and the arrow of victory over Aram; for you will defeat the Arameans at Aphek until you have put an end to *them*.' Then he said, 'Take the arrows,' and he took *them*. And he said to the king of Israel, 'Strike the ground,' and he struck it three times and stopped. Then the man of God became angry at him and said, 'You should have struck five or six times, then you would have struck Aram until you put an end to *it*. But now you shall strike Aram only three times.'
>
> And Elisha died, and they buried him. Now the marauding bands of the Moabites would invade the land in the spring of the year.
>
> (2 Kings 13:14-20, NASB)

What a crazy story! Why did Elisha become so angry at the king for only striking the arrow three times? The king seemed to follow Elisha's oddly specific instructions pretty well. What are we missing? What did the king miss that ultimately cost him lasting success and staying power as a leader?

To find out, you need to go beyond the words of the text into the emotion of this story. The enemy is relentless and again closing in. The king knows he has limited time with this ailing prophet, so he goes to him again, perhaps looking for a blessing and an easy fix. As he goes through Elisha's instructions, it's not hard to imagine the king being annoyed and maybe impatient. ***Let's get on with this already.*** And when he strikes the arrow only three times, the old prophet comes unglued and tells the king he will have only partial victory. God's blessing would not be complete. Ultimately the Moabites would win the day.

So what is the king missing? If Joash truly embraced the moment and what was at stake, if he knew this might be the last time he was in the presence of this seasoned man of God, would he have acted so rushed? Would he have struck that arrow only three times? If he were fully in that moment, would he not have struck it with fiery passion five or six times or many more? I can feel it as I write. Those arrows should have been struck with force and intensity. Striking the arrow only three times almost seems like the king is bored and just going through the motions.

Passion is clearly missing in this story—a fire in the gut that says we will move forward. Life is short, the stakes high, and our mission too compelling not to see it all the way through.

God has used many different things to ignite my passion and re-engage me in the wild pursuit of him. Inspiring moments in the movies *Gladiator*, *The Secret Life of Walter Mitty*, and so many others. Or hearing Marcus Mumford sing "Grace" and "Awake my Soul." Bono crying out that he still hasn't found what he's looking for, or hearing Tom Petty in one of his last concerts before he passed say, we will keep swinging until one of us drops. All these moments and so many more served to re-ignite a passionate, wild pursuit of God and all he has for me.

Part of what *Jesus Revolution* did was wake me up and remind me that this spiritual journey we're on is real and the stakes are high. It reminded me that no matter how dark or divided this country gets, no matter how fast this culture runs from God, no matter how much success we may enjoy or how discouraging the obstacles and disappointments, even if a physical enemy takes its toll, no matter how much I may struggle with the same screw-ups and mistakes, God can still work powerfully through my broken story and flawed leadership. I just need to pay attention and not forget the powerful stories and ways God has already shown up. I need to stay passionate, remembering those thin place moments when heaven and earth have collided and offered me a glimpse of God and who he is. Those moments can be the fuel that keeps me moving forward no matter what.

## Chapter 15: To the Edge

I wonder if one of the first things we must shed in a disrupted world is our expectations. Because the world is not predictable. It's dynamic. The status quo will no longer get us where we want to go. To remain on this wild adventure, we must be ready for anything, even those things that make no sense.

When we started Harbor Ministries more than fifteen years ago, it didn't make much sense. We wanted to be about something that would bring deep, transformative change in the lives of leaders. We wanted to launch a movement that would have not just local but national impact. And we were fiercely committed to doing that just twenty leaders at a time. No large groups, big rallies, or flashy speakers. Those things all have a place, but we felt called to something different. We wanted to change the leadership narrative and have a footprint of influence that would stretch coast to coast by taking the slow route and deeply investing in twenty leaders at a time in each group over two or three years.

I remember our early meeting with a national magazine in Orlando, Florida. We wanted to get ourselves on the map but we had zero track record and limited finances. We were about to spend a sizable chunk of what we did have on an ad in their magazine. They didn't get it. It made no sense to them that we would take out a full-page ad to attract twenty people. They thought we were crazy. We thought we were crazy, but we had this conviction that if we can get the right twenty people in the room, we can change the leadership story and have an impact on the crisis in leadership in this country. So many times through the years, others talked to us about scaling the ministry, expanding, doing more. I felt pressed to grow the numbers, go bigger, go faster. We did launch more groups but held to this vision that investing radically in twenty at a time could change everything.

Fast forward a decade, and I'm sitting in a meeting of strategic Christian leaders in the Tampa Bay/St. Petersburg area. Twelve CEOs and corporate leaders from large organizations in the area sat around the table. I took a deep breath as I looked around the room and realized half the group had been through one of our leadership journeys. I fought back emotion as each man described the impact Harbor and the ROGUE leadership journey had on their stories, their families, and the organizations they led. The footprint and influence of Harbor had spread through central Florida. I called one of the guys who started this whole thing with me. "It's happening," I said. "We have no idea how far and how deep the influence and impact of what God is doing has spread."

Sometimes God calls us into things that make no sense. But don't worry; we're in good company. Gideon is an ordinary guy who shows up in the book of Judges. He has no special lineage or background, no leadership resume. He lives in a cave with his small family—a very ordinary guy whose world is about to explode. So what went through Gideon's mind when God said he would lead the Hebrews to victory against a far superior enemy?

*God, are you sure? You know this makes no sense, right?*

Then after Gideon is embraced as a leader of the Hebrew people, God takes it even further and lays out a crazy plan for how Gideon will lead the people to an impossible win against a massive force. God invites Gideon and the Hebrew people into a bigger story that demonstrates he is the God of second and third chances. Let's set the scene: Fierce people have been terrorizing the Hebrew people. Now they have banded together into a large force with one intent: destroy Gideon's small army and wipe out the Hebrew people. Sounds bad. But God tells Gideon he will lead the army against the Midianite force that stretches as far as the eye can see.

*God, are you sure? You know this makes no sense, right?*

Then God gives Gideon the battle plan. First, He will reduce Gideon's army from 32,0000 to 10,000 and then to 300! Those 300 will go against the Midianites and defeat them.

*Um, okay. You know this makes no sense, right?*

Here is how it went down:

> 'Therefore, tell the people, 'Whoever is timid or afraid may leave the mountain and go home.' So 22,000 of them went home, leaving only 10,000 who were willing to fight. But the Lord told Gideon, 'There are still too many! Bring them down to the spring, and I will test them to determine who will go with you and who will not.' When Gideon took the warriors to the water the Lord told him, 'Divide the men into two groups. In one group put all those who cup water in their hands and lap it up with their tongues like dogs. In the other group put all those who kneel down and drink with their mouths in the stream.' Only 300 of the men drank with their hands. . . . The Lord told Gideon, 'With these 300 men I will rescue you and give victory over the Midianites.'
>
> (Judges 7:3-7 NLT)

*Sorry, but what?*

How many of us are signing up for this one? And what is with the lapping water out of their hands like a dog thing? After I preached on this story a while back, a man in the military approached me and said, "You know why they did that, right? It is a sign of readiness, water brought up to their face. They never lost sight of what was in front of them and around them. They were ready, alert, aware." Each of the 300 men God sent into battle with Gideon was ready. They were prepared to fight the Midianites. Maybe it did make sense.

Courage was the first qualifier in the story, and following God today—especially today—takes steady resolve and courage! "Whoever is timid or afraid may leave the mountain and go home." (Judges 7:3, NLT)

Leadership also plays an undeniable role in the story. Gideon was just a common man, nothing special about his story. One way or another, we are all in positions of influence and leadership, so we must be listening, alert, ready, and watching, not losing sight of what is happening around us or what is important, not losing sight of the bigger story.

God also set up this story so that only he gets the credit. See verse two:

> The Lord said to Gideon, 'You have too many warriors with you. If I let all of you fight the Midianites, the Israelites will boast to me that they saved themselves by their own strength.'
>
> (Judges 7:2, NLT)

God could have ended this himself, but as he has throughout history, he worked through men and women. He invites us into the story, and, at moments, he calls us into things and places that stretch us, force us into risk, and sometimes make no sense. The

May 30th entry in *My Utmost for His Highest* asks us to consider how we will respond when that happens.

> Suppose God calls you to do something that is an enormous test of your common sense, totally going against it. What will you do? Will you hold back?
>
> . . . we tend to say, 'Yes, but—suppose I do obey God in the matter, what about . . .' Or we say, 'Yes, I will obey God if what He asks of me doesn't go against my common sense, but don't ask me to take a step in the dark.'
>
> . . . If a person is ever going to do anything worthwhile, there will be times when he must risk everything by his leap in the dark . . . Once you obey, you will find that what he says is as solidly consistent as common sense.[5]

As the story of Gideon continues, we see that God doesn't send Gidian into the moment blind. He gives him confirmation, encouragement, and an inspired plan.

That night the Lord said, 'Get up! Go down into the Midianite camp, for I have given you victory over them. But if you are afraid to attack, go down to the camp with your servant Purah. Listen to what the Midianites are saying, and you will be greatly encouraged.' (Judges 7:9-11, NLT)

On the surface, God's plan looks crazy. Send most of your warriors home. Use trumpets and lanterns instead of weapons. Attack at night. It's not crazy; it's cunning. The plan creates chaos, camels stampede, and panic permeates among the Midianites, who flee in fear and confusion.

When this story began, personal safety was no guarantee. God only promised that Gideon would defeat the Midianites and he would be with them.

So what are some of the challenges you face?

How can you best position yourself to be ready when challenges arise?

In the past, how have you found a rhythm and a plan to help you through a challenging time?

When you think of someone who has stepped into something that seemed crazy at the time, what did you observe about them? How did they navigate it, and what were some of the results of the steps they took?

Yes, there are times God will call us to go outside conventional wisdom and common sense. In some ways, that is the essence of the faith journey. Those can be the moments we come alive and become dangerous again. But this kind of wild living takes enduring courage, a steely resolve, and a willingness to step into the unknown—even when it makes no sense.

## Chapter 16: Strip Down

One of my goals has been to hike this trail between Aspen and Crested Butte, Colorado. The popular ski towns are close to 100 miles apart by road, but if you're up for adventure, you can hike over the 12,500-foot West Maroon Pass. It's seventeen miles long, and one of the big challenges of this hike, besides the Rocky Mountain terrain, is logistics. Getting to the trailhead and arranging transportation can be a hurdle unless you make it a roundtrip. Even though I've talked about doing this hike many times over the years, I've yet to make it happen.

A few years back, I heard about a guy with a much bigger goal. He wanted to hike the Colorado Trail. Being in his sixties, he knew the window was closing, so he planned, trained, and set out on his adventure. It wasn't easy. The trail runs across the Rocky Mountains from south of Denver to Durango. It is 486 miles and has an elevation gain of 89,000 feet. Despite wanting to give up many times, he finished this hike in thirty-six days. "It's amazing what you can accomplish by just taking the next step," he said.

He faced three significant challenges on his journey that nearly took him out: weather, isolation, and the weight he carried with him. He could not control the weather, and it proved a relentless foe. Many days, he never saw the sun, and if I remember his story correctly, he had a multiday stretch of constant rain, sleet, or snow. He spent each night trying to get dry, only to wake up and face the elements again. The weather tested his spirit, body, and will in every way.

He rarely saw other hikers on the trail. He had arranged to see his wife at strategic points along the route to replenish his supplies,

but other than those times, he was alone. More than a month of isolation and the intense loneliness that followed nearly took him out.

One thing he could control was the weight of what he carried. He was meticulous about planning the weight to the ounce. He carried only the absolute essentials. He was so committed to traveling as lightly as possible I was told he even cut off part of his toothbrush. Every ounce mattered. He was convinced that the cumulative effect of carrying too much weight would derail his journey.

As we intentionally choose the wild path, we'd be wise to consider the impact of weather, weight, and loneliness over the long haul. We can't do much about the weather other than prepare as best we can and be ready to adjust our plans. One thing we know for sure in this life, things will change and most certainly go differently than we thought. But, the elements of isolation and weight—we can have some impact on those.

In my book *Thin Places*, I talked about the perfect storm that had formed in my life in my early forties. I was leading a large organization with a dynamic staff and a compelling mission. But there were cracks in the armor that were starting to emerge. I now describe it as a perfect storm of fatigue, boredom, and disappointment. Like so many of us in this season of life, I was carrying so much weight with family, marriage, growing a ministry, raising funds, and so many other issues. Then disappointments and boredom began to set in and take a stronghold. I'm guessing many of you reading this can relate in one way or another. This may be a good time to journal some on that.

How do fatigue, disappointment, and boredom factor in at work?

In your marriage?

In your relationship with God?

Be honest with yourself and God. Maybe bring a trusted friend into this as well.

One of the mistakes I made at that point in my life was that I isolated myself from others on the serious issues. I had good family and friend relationships, but I was not letting anyone in on the deeper, more difficult questions, and I had a hard time finding the right words for what I was feeling. I have been leading ministry organizations and nonprofits my entire adult life, and it's often been hard to let others in. When I was at the head of a large Youth for Christ chapter that was having a significant impact, I was struggling, doubting God, and experiencing some depression and discouragement. I felt trapped. Who could I tell? The young staff who was looking to me for encouragement and inspiration? My board of directors that included many friends who were also donors to our organization? My wife, who needed me to be strong in the middle of the demands of raising a family? I isolated myself instead of taking a risk and sharing my struggles with others. At one of the most impacting times of my life, surrounded by so many people and engaged in so many relationships, I still felt lonely.

And boredom—that was real to me once I was able to name it. I finally spoke the words, "I think I'm bored at work and in relationships." Only when I was willing to name it could I get to a place to do something about it.

And soon, the excess weight I was carrying from that perfect storm began to take a toll. Hebrews 12 tells us to throw off everything that hinders us so that we can run the race. The Message says it this way:

> Do you see what this means—all these pioneers who blazed the way, all these veterans cheering us on? It means we better get on with it. Strip down, start running—and never quit! No extra spiritual fat, no parasitic sins. Keep your eyes on Jesus, who both began and finished this race we're in. Study how he did it. Because he never lost sight of where he was headed—that exhilarating finish in and with God.
>
> (Hebrews 12:1-2, MSG)

Let's stay with the passage for a while. Reread it slowly.

Who were some of those pioneers who blazed the trail in your life? Maybe it was someone close or someone who mentored or invested in you from afar. Get out your journal. Name them and describe the impact they had on your life. Don't forget. If they are still with us, this may be a good time to drop them a note.

And how about that idea of veterans cheering you on? What do you think of that? Do you believe it? In your mind's eye, picture yourself running a marathon, and all along the route are people cheering, encouraging, exhorting you to keep moving to the finish line. I do take this passage literally. I believe a cloud of witnesses is cheering you on, believing you have what it takes, telling you you've got this, to keep going, live in the moment, and take the next step.

Then, this is a great time to ask God to reveal what you're carrying that you need to throw off. Is there some boredom, apathy, disappointment, pride, or anger that has set in? Is there a habit, some damaging self-talk, a relationship, or a structure you need to cast off to lighten your load? This passage is not just talking about the dark stuff that many of us carry—it says to let go of anything that is slowing you down, blocking a relationship with God, or hindering a strong finish.

> Strip down, start running—and never quit!
>
> No extra spiritual fat, no parasitic sins.
>
> Keep your eyes on *Jesus*, who both began and finished this race we're in. Study how he did it.
>
> Because he never lost sight of where he was headed—that exhilarating finish in and with God.
>
> (Hebrews 12:1-2, MSG)

If we plan to stay in the game for the long haul, if we are to have a shot of finishing life and our journey with God well, we must carry a very light load and take only the absolute necessities with us. In my early twenties, I took some friends on a backpacking trip in Colorado. None of us were very experienced, and the trail we were going on would be tough. At the grocery store, I remember telling everyone to pack light. As we readied ourselves to hit the trail, one of the guys pulled out a huge can of pork and beans and a cantaloupe. After some relentless joking, I took the cantaloupe and heaved it off the mountain. I still remember that melon shattering on a rock below, as well as the look on my friend's face. He seemed poised to take a swing at me. I didn't want the heavy load of one person to potentially ruin the hike for all of us. Maybe I could have thought of another way to handle it, but it created a memory and a story I'm still telling years later.

Even our emotions and theology sometimes need to be stripped down. I've been friends with another one of the guys on that hike for more than forty years. Back in college, we had spirited debates on all kinds of theology and political issues. Free will vs. predestination was one of our favorite topics. It could get intense. He was a pastor for years, and just a few months ago, he told me, "I am sure of much less today than ever." And that's true for me as well. Things that seemed so important all those years ago just don't matter as much anymore. So I am sticking to the absolute core of my faith and taking only the basics with me. I am leaving my judgments and strong emotions around the secondary issues of the faith behind. Those are hills not worth dying on, and they will eventually take care of themselves. I'm taking only the absolute essentials for this next stretch of the journey.

A determined resolve to stay light is vital. I think of two moments when Jesus invited others to follow him. One was the rich young ruler whose story is told in Mark 10. He asks Jesus what he must do to follow him, and Jesus tells him to sell his possessions, give to the poor, and follow him. Simple, profound, but difficult to follow, especially when you are carrying a lot with you. The passage says the rich young ruler had much, and the ask was too big. He could not let go, and we never heard of him again.

When Jesus invites Peter to follow him, Peter drops his nets. It was no small thing to drop the tools of his livelihood, walk away from the family business, leave his father, and follow Jesus, but he did. He cast everything aside and was ready to go. A simple, profound, difficult moment that changed everything.

We turn again to Hebrews 12.

> Strip down, start running—and never quit! No extra spiritual fat, no parasitic sins. Keep your eyes on *Jesus*, who both began and finished this race we're in. Study how he did it. Because

he never lost sight of where he was headed—that exhilarating finish in and with God.

(Hebrews 12:1-2, MSG)

The words are compelling and clear. Lighten up. These times we live in require us to let go of the things that are dragging us down, slowing us, and making us ineffective. God may ask us to follow him down another path at any moment. Are you in a position and state of mind to follow him? Don't get stuck on the things that divide and don't matter. Life is too short to get caught up, lose friends, and push people into separate camps. The last verse in Psalm 46 that we explored earlier comes to mind: "Step out of the traffic! Take a long, loving look at me, your High God, above politics, above everything." (Psalm 46:10, MSG)

Are you ready to do that? Can you let go of the politics and some of the divisive issues of our day that are driving people away from the Christian faith? Can you let go of some of the very good things you are carrying so you can engage in the great stuff?

Does anything else come to mind that you need to let go of so you are ready? No extra spiritual fat. No parasitic sins. With that lighter load, we are positioned well to adjust, change, shift, and move when the weather changes.

## The Wind

We can't leave the topic of weather without talking about the wind. The wind is a disruptor. It can wear on you and cause you to alter plans, adjust, or change directions, sometimes without warning. It can be hard, soothing, refreshing, wild, and unpredictable.

I was in San Diego preparing for one of our leadership events. I had a couple of hours before the first meeting, so I rented a bike and hit the road in Coronado, heading south. I love to bike and knew I needed to exercise before this event kicked off, so I was enjoying the ride. With the sights and sounds of the ocean to my right, my adrenaline really kicked in. I was riding hard and fast. Well into the ride, I made the turn to head back and get to the meeting on time. It was a discouraging reality. Not once had I thought about the wind that was pushing me down the coastline. Now, I had to fight the wind. I hadn't accounted for or adjusted to the wind, and the price was high. It was a battle all the way back. I was exhausted, and my legs were mush. I spent much of the grueling ride engaging in positive self-talk:

*You idiot.*

*You're going to be so late.*

*How did you not think about this or account for this?*

Wind can change everything.

The Bible often refers to God as the holy wind. The disciples gathered after Jesus's death, not knowing their next steps. They wondered what their lives would be like from that point forward. Would they be killed or not make it through another night? Then, they got the news that Jesus was alive. And it says the Holy Spirit

came as a wind that blew through and filled their sails. After that, none of them would be the same.

Acts 2:3 says, "without warning there was a sound like a strong wind, gale force—no one could tell where it came from. It filled the whole building. Then, like a wildfire, the Holy Spirit spread through their ranks . . ." (Acts 2:2, MSG). Everything changed.

Revelation 3 invites us to listen for this holy wind: "Are your ears awake? Listen. Listen to the Wind Words, the Spirit blowing through the churches." (Revelation 3:6, MSG)

Clearly, we can't control the wind. We can't dictate it or change it, but we can ready ourselves to respond to it when it comes. I recently heard a podcast by John Eldredge where he listed four items that are useless at sea: a rudder, oars, an anchor, and the fear of going down. Out on the sea, direction is determined by currents and wind.

A wild man becomes a crazy man when he doesn't respect the wind but fights against it. But a wild man reads the wind and understands that it will change. He is ready to embrace it, despite the risks. He readies for the changes and shifts as needed. He listens and responds to wherever the wind may take him.

John 3:8 says, "The wind blows wherever it pleases. You hear its sound, but you cannot tell where it comes from or where it is going. So it is with everyone born of the Spirit." (John 3:8, NIV) The Greek word ***pneuma***, used in this passage, can mean spirit, breath, or wind.

What would it look like for you to release some control, make some adjustments, and see where the holy wind takes you?

To stay on this wild pursuit of God, we had better face the realities of loneliness, weather, and weight. When we have, we're in a much better place to have the steely resolve necessary to keep going.

## Chapter 17: Out of the Ruts

> But forget all that—it is nothing compared to what I am going to do.
>
> For I'm about to do something new. See, I have already begun it. Do you not see it?
>
> I will make a pathway through the wilderness.
>
> (Isaiah 43:18-19, NLT)

About seven miles from the farmhouse I grew up in, you'll find remnants of the Oregon Trail. There are places you can see the pathway where all those wagons crossed the prairie more than 150 years ago. In that part of south-central Nebraska, every wagon train followed this path, leaving marks that are still visible today. There was good reason to follow in the ruts of the wagons that had gone before. The path had been scouted out and offered the safest, most predictable route. Sticking to those ruts offered the pioneers some understanding of what lay ahead.

My great-grandfather arrived in Nebraska on one of those wagons. He brought his wife and sons with him. But there was a moment when he decided to leave the safety of those ruts and veer south. Whatever his reasons, he set out on his own. He stopped several miles south in the middle of endless grassland, planted a few trees to claim the land, and built a sod house to give his family shelter. He took an incredible risk by leaving the safety of routine and the company of others. He left those ruts. His decision has impacted generations. The farm he settled in the middle of the absolute unknown is still blessing his family nearly 150 years later. That's incredible.

I have learned from those pioneers who have gone before me. It's not just important, but essential, to listen, study, and hear from those who have walked this road before. We'd be fools not to do that. Learning from the pioneers and following their paths for a time is critical to teaching us how to navigate life. We glean wisdom from observing those who have gone before us and faced similar obstacles and struggles.

*But . . .*

There are times when we need to veer left or right and step into the unknown. There are moments when we must take a risk, and our only assurance is that God will walk with us. This is the essence of the faith journey. There are moments when we need to enter the unknown, breathe in new air, and, for a time, step out alone. There is no other way to do it.

Stepping out of the ruts is risky.

It's scary.

It's life-giving.

I'm not sure of all the dynamics that drove my great-grandfather, but he was clearly not content to settle or coast. Instead, he pursued mystery, wonder, adventure, and risk. He willingly put it all on the line to make something new in the wilderness. I hope I would have done the same.

More than a decade ago, we launched Harbor Ministries. We broke out of the ruts of the traditional ministry models of the day and invited just twenty at a time into a different kind of journey—something transformational, something that creates space for strategic leaders to listen. We believed that if we stayed committed

to that principle over the long haul, we could eventually change the world. All these years later, as I travel to places like Los Angeles, Phoenix, Dallas, Denver, St. Petersburg, Tampa Bay, Virginia Beach, Knoxville, Minneapolis, Lincoln, and so many others, to visit those who have been through one of our leadership journeys, I believe that more than ever.

All those years ago, it took a dream to be the catalyst for change, and the calling that followed drove me to turn off the beaten path and try something new. I was told we could not sustain or fund this kind of model. We had no guarantees, and I put my time and resources, and the time and resources of many others, at risk in the process. But I knew it was time to try something new. I had to turn aside from the safe and predictable. I had to take the chance. I don't want to lose that edge. No matter how old I am, I don't want to get stuck in a rut and just coast.

When Henry Bohlke turned off the beaten path, I imagine he had many of the same thoughts I had when we started Harbor.

> *Am I putting my family and everything I own and love at risk?*
>
> *What if this doesn't work?*
>
> *What if we die out in this prairie, and no one ever knows?*
>
> *Should I stay in the safety of others and this well-used path and see what happens?*

We too often listen to the wrong voices. *That's too risky. That makes no sense. You're too old. You're too young. It's safer away from the edge. Settle in. You deserve to coast for a while. That's too much work. It will cost too much. Head over heart. It needs to make sense. That will never work. You don't have the right education or life experience. Act your age.*

All those things that crossed his mind (and later mine) were accurate. They could have died. They very likely could have failed, and if they had failed, who would ever know? People probably did think they were crazy.

I remember the months leading up to the first Harbor event. Would anyone apply, and if they applied and were accepted, when it came right down to it, would they show up? The night before the event in Estes Park was a mix of excitement and nagging questions. Why would leaders from around the country fly in to meet with leaders they'd never heard of? One guy's wife warned him that we were probably a cult. There was a very significant chance it would all end in utter failure, yet there was something energizing about that time. I was deeply reflective and highly dependent on God. I was dialed in. That place of high risk and utter discomfort brought out the best in me. It still does.

Today, a century and a half after Henry left the ruts, his legacy helped fund the Harbor story. The farmstead he first planted continues to bless my family to this day. The income of that farm has multiplied to three families and has given me the margin over the years that allowed me to stay in vocational ministry. I am so thankful for his pioneering, risk-taking spirit. As you read this section and something is stirring, one thing you can do is find the SPACE podcast by Harbor Ministries and listen to episode 91: "These are the Pioneers."

With the years I have left, I want to wisely follow the beaten path when I should but remain alert, ready, and willing to turn out of the ruts. I hope that for you as well. May you have the wisdom to learn from those who have gone before us, the peace to stay in the ruts when you need to, and the courage and strength to turn and forge a new path when God leads.

*The cowards never started, the weak died along the way, only the strong survived. They were the pioneers. -Author Unknown*

## Chapter 18: Stay as Long as It Takes

During this new, disrupted reality, I've been drawn to the story of Elijah. Elijah is God's chosen prophet during a very dark time in the history of the Hebrew people. The people and their leaders have again turned away from God and turned to false prophets and idol gods, specifically the idol god Baal. So God sends Elijah to warn the king to turn back to the one true God, but the king refuses. What follows is two and a half years of drought. The people are suffering, and Elijah pleads with God on their behalf. This is such a cool part of this story. Elijah intercedes on behalf of the people, and his passionate prayers have an impact.

So God sent Elijah back to the king to give him another shot. And after a series of events, Elijah single-handedly kills the false prophets of the day—well over 100 of them! Now I don't know all that happened to bring him to the point, but no matter how we feel about it, that's an intense, over-the-top response from this wild man in the desert.

When the queen, who is fiercely committed to Baal, learns what Elijah has done, she sends him a message, basically saying that by the following night, Elijah will be as dead as her prophets. So what happens to this man of courage who has twice gone toe-to-toe with the king, interceded for the people, and slain the prophets?

When we pick up the story in 1 Kings 19, Elijah is depleted, struggling with exhaustion, discouragement, and even fear. And he is running for his life. He has completely extended himself, given everything he has, and it isn't enough. Elijah's at great risk of not finishing well. Alone and disillusioned, tired, weary, mentally, spiritually, and emotionally spent, he finds himself under a tree in a desert, ready to give up.

I found myself in one of those places a few years ago. We were walking through some hard stuff with a couple of our kids, and I was carrying so much on their behalf. I had tried everything to help them in this very dark season. I was disappointed in God, hurting for them, and really struggling as a result. On one particularly difficult day, I decided to go for a ride on my mountain bike. That bike helped me get through a lot of dark days. Riding is fun and pure therapy for me. I really needed both that day.

I decided to ride to a church a few miles from my house with a simple bench and prayer fountain, where I frequently found myself that summer. I had been training my dog to run alongside the bike, but this day she decided to cut in front of me, which caused me to crash and grind my face on the asphalt. Undeterred, I took her back home and headed for that bench and prayer fountain alone. Just as I sat down, a nest of wasps exploded from the bottom of that bench and hammered me. You really can't make this stuff up.

I ripped off my shirt and yelled at those wasps. "You think this hurts? This is nothing! Bring it!"

I have thought often about that day. I wonder what people thought as they watched this crazy man scream at those wasps. In some ways, it was the moment I hit the bottom, when I realized there was nothing I could do to fix things. It was time for me to surrender control—or any control I thought I had—and give up the outcomes I had hoped for. Once again, I had to decide if I believed what I had preached all these years. Would I follow God and trust him, or would I cave in despair?

It was close.

So back to Elijah, how does God meet him in that desperate moment under that tree? God lets Elijah sleep and then gives him food and water, and not just a little bread and water. The text says bread cooked over hot coals and a pitcher of water. It's a picture of abundance. God lets him sleep again. Then after Elijah is rested and well-fed, he invites him to the mountain. God asks Elijah to stay alert and promises that he will meet him there, that he will pass by. Elijah reaches Mount Horeb and sleeps in a cave. Then an angel comes and asks Elijah what he is doing there.

> And he said, 'I have been very zealous for the Lord, the God of armies; for the sons of Israel have abandoned Your covenant, torn down Your altars, and killed Your prophets with the sword. And I alone am left; and they have sought to take my life.'
>
> (1 Kings 19:10, NASB)

Elijah pours out his heart, and how does God respond? Does he tell him to buck up? Does he say to move on and stop whining? Does he lecture him on having enough faith in this moment? What does God ask of Elijah at this critical moment?

> So He said, 'Go out and stand on the mountain at attention before the Lord.' And behold, the Lord was passing by! And a great and powerful wind was tearing out the mountains and breaking the rocks in pieces before the Lord; *but* the Lord was not in the wind. And after the wind *there was* an earthquake, *but* the Lord was not in the earthquake. And after the earthquake, a fire, *but* the Lord was not in the fire; and after the fire, a sound of a gentle blowing.
>
> (1 Kings 19:11-12, NASB)

Another translation says, "and after the fire came a gentle, quiet whisper." And after this whisper, God asks Elijah again, "Why are you here?" This time, Elijah is ready to answer, and you sense he has a different resolve.

Let's process this story. First, let's recognize that God met Elijah in a dark place. Elijah was exhausted and out of hope. What God doesn't do is say, "What's wrong with you that you don't have enough faith? Suck it up! Don't you know what others have gone through? This is nothing!" No, he doesn't say any of that. Instead, he first meets Elijah with food, water, and rest . . . and an invitation to be honest.

Then, God invites Elijah to the mountain and asks him to stay there as long as it takes for God to pass by. A hurricane rips through the mountain and shatters the rocks, but God is not in the wind. Then comes an earthquake and fire, but God is in neither. Then God shows up in a gentle, quiet whisper.

How long did all of this take? It surely wasn't an hour or even a day. Elijah was likely on that mountain at attention before God for a long time, maybe days or even weeks. We know there is history on this mountain. Moses waited for God for forty days. But God did show up—for Moses and now for Elijah.

He'll show up for us, too.

After all of this, after good food, good drink, and a crazy great thin place moment, God asks Elijah again why he is there. And then, at the end of 1 Kings 19, God gives Elijah encouragement, strength, and clarity for his final mission.

So where are you at in this story?

Do you need rest, good food, or a good drink?

Do you need permission to get honest and name how you're doing and how you feel about God and this journey you are on? Is there some disappointment you need to name?

Is there a nagging sense that you are not enough, that you've tried a lot of things and it's just not good enough?

Do you need some clarity on the next season of your journey? Do you just need to be reminded that God will pass by?

The calling of this story—the whisper that reaches us still in this fully disrupted world—is that wherever we are, no matter what, there will be a moment. He will pass by if we are willing to go to the mountain and stay there.

The key is to stay.

In January 2009, I explored the risks of not keeping my heart and mind open to wild new adventures. I share part of that entry as a closing thought:

> *This morning I was prompted to read some of my journal entries over the last year. The theme was all about movement and taking steps of faith that are way bigger than me, taking steps toward the people and things God seems to be calling to. As I look at some of my journal entries, it seems like there is way more risk in staying safe and comfortable. When I have not taken some risk, my heart deadens, and my emotions and life seem to flatten. It's kind of wild that some fear, risk, and even a chance of failure somehow energize and mobilize me to action.*
>
> *In early 2008 I wrote, 'I have to be willing to step into opportunities that God seems to be giving me. I must listen, yes,*

*weigh the costs and assess the risk but not be so careful that I don't move. I've got to be willing to take the first step, and then the dominos will fall. Small first steps can bring huge outcomes and significant consequences. And maybe the worst consequences are if I don't at least try. One small act of courage, like launching this first-ever RHYTHMinTWENTY group with Harbor, could actually start a movement and deeply impact the lives of so many. I really do believe that. If I wait for absolute certainty and affirmation of taking these steps in front of me, I may miss the moment. Even though this adventure of Harbor may fail miserably, I wonder if ten years from now I'm more likely to be haunted by the fact that I failed or more by the regret that I did not give this a shot.' (March 8, 2008, journal entry)*

*So as I think about 2009, I wonder what risk, even reckless steps await me that I should take. In relationships, in Harbor Ministries, in family, in my personal life, in my relationship with God, what opportunities is God moving my heart toward? I do know that thinking about them is not enough. I must be willing to step out.*

*In days gone by, ships would have to wait for high tide and not miss that moment to enter the harbor. I read this Shakespeare quote that says, "There is a tide in the affairs of men, Which taken at the flood, leads on to fortune. Omitted, all the voyage of their life is bound in shallows and in miseries. On such a full sea are we now afloat. And we must take the current when it serves, or lose our ventures."*[6]

*I can't live with any more what-if questions. I have had too many of those in my past. I need to stay when I need to stay, but be ready to move even if it looks reckless or crazy to some. Here is to taking the steps I need to in the coming year.*

-January 9, 2009 Journal Entry

So here's the invitation:

Stay.

Stay wild.

## References

[1] Dallas Willard, *The Spirit of the Disciplines: Understanding How God Changes Lives,* New York: Harper Collins, 1998.

[2] Jonathan Cahn, *The Book of Mysteries,* Lake Mary, FL: Charisma House, 2018, p 8.

[3] Michael Easter, *The Comfort Crisis: Embrace Discomfort to Reclaim Your Wild, Happy, Healthy Self,* New York: Rodale Books, 2021, pp 128,129.

[4] Easter, *Comfort Crisis*, p 5.

[5] Oswald Chambers, *My Utmost for His Highest: Updated Edition,* Grand Rapids, MI: Discovery House Publishers,1992, May 30th entry.

[6] William Shakespeare, Julius Caesar (London: First Folio, 1623), Act IV.

## Images

Why:

Matt Howard on Unsplash

Chapter 3:

Juli Kosolapova on Unsplash

Holly Mandarich on Unsplash

Chapter 5:

Pine Watt on Unsplash

Chapter 10:

Matt Howard on Unsplash

Chapter 13:

Kirill Tonkikh on Unsplash

Chapter 16:

Michael Kirsh on Unsplash

Thom Milkovic on Unsplash

Nathan Anderson on Unsplash

Chapter 17:

Tyler Costa Photography via Shutterstock

Other photos from Harbor photographers: Brooke Confer, Ben Harms, and John Wooton

## Music

Music Lyrics by Bryan Olesen of Harbor Ministries

## Resources

### Books

*Harbor Seven: Thoughts on the Journey from a Man Well-traveled* by Tim Bohlke

*Thin Places* by Tim Bohlke

*Field Guide for SPACE* from Harbor Ministries

### Podcast

The SPACE Podcast is available on Spotify, Apple Podcasts, and Google Podcasts

For more information and resources, visit HarborMinistries.com

### Music

Original music is written by Harbor's Bryan Olesen and performed by Vota. For more information, visit HarborMinistries.com and VotaBand.com.